Shifra Stein's

A Kid's Guide
to
Kansas City

HARROW BOOKS
Kansas City, Missouri

Also by Shifra Stein:

The All-American Barbecue Book (with Rich Davis)
Discover Kansas City
Kansas City: A Unique Guide to the Metro Area
The Edible City
Day Trips: Kansas City
Day Trips: Baltimore
Day Trips: Houston
Day Trips: Phoenix-Tucson-Flagstaff
Day Trips: St. Louis
Day Trips: Minneapolis/St. Paul
Day Trips: Cincinnati

Shifra Stein's A Kid's Guide to Kansas City
First Printing May, 1989
Second Printing July, 1989

©1989 by Shifra Stein

ISBN Number: 0-916455-02-5
Library of Congress Catalog Card Number: 89-084106

Printed in the United States of America

Dedication

To Jason, who always says that kids
are just as important as adults.

Table of Contents

ACKNOWLEDGMENTS

A KID'S GUIDE TO KANSAS CITY would not have been possible without the dedication of researchers who helped with this project. Several parents wanted very much to be a part of this community effort. They researched attractions and activities they felt would be suitable for their own kids.

Certainly all those who worked on this publication have an affinity for children, and possess a keen ability to ferret out the kinds of things parents need to know. So it is with great affection and appreciation that we thank **Marli Murphy, Liz White, Kathy Hamilton, Sally Sebeckis, Antionette Vigliaturo Ishmael, Meredith Schraeder, Marty Porter, Linda Rodriguez, Mary Spitcaufsky,** and **Roy Gunter,** who helped transform an idea into reality.

INTRODUCTION

Books are like children. They start with a gleam in the eye, take about nine months to develop, and then they're born.

The actual idea for A KID'S GUIDE TO KANSAS CITY came from some area parents who complained that there was nothing like this publication available on the shelves. Since I'm always looking for an available gap to fill, I ran the idea by Roy Gunter, former President of the National Education Association of Shawnee Mission, Kansas. He liked it and agreed to facilitate a series of meetings with PTA groups, which were most helpful and assertive about what the publication should include.

PTA parents agreed that the book should be laid out according to *location,* rather than by *category.* It would have been easy, for example, to lump all area museums into one section, as most area guides tend to do. But as one mother pointed out: "If I drive all the way out to Independence to see the Truman Library with my 5-year-old, I sure want to know what else there is to do around there."

So, in addition to other nearby attractions, we added area parks where children could play, restaurants that catered to kids, and, above all, the location of the nearest rest room. (When we phoned key personnel to ask whether or not their facilities offered educational and cultural experiences as well as toilets, this provoked many a surprised response!)

It took a while to collate everything from museums, parks, and restaurants to neighborhood tours, amusements and sports, and stick them individually within their appropriate neighborhood.

Space limitations prevented us from listing some of the finer dining establishments that cater to families. However we wanted to include just a few quick-stop spots for parents on the go with kids in tow.

We also included some of the available accommodations for the disabled. However, we lack space to give a complete breakdown of all facilities, so we recommend that you check with an organization such as The Whole Person, Inc., (listed in this book) for complete details.

For the most part, age suitability of the child was recommended by the business, attraction, or agency itself. Parents, of course, can use their own discretion. We can advise that a night at the opera might be more appropriate for older children, but have no way of knowing if there's a toddler out there who can actually sit through an entire performance of Puccini without visiting the bathroom more than once. So we have to leave the final decision up to you as to whether or not your youngster is ready for many of the experiences mentioned in this book.

Business hours are frequently subject to change, so we've included phone numbers to call for the latest up-to-date information.

As you read through A KID'S GUIDE TO KANSAS CITY, we hope you'll be as delighted as we were to discover what the city has to offer. We were astounded by the number of fine arts organizations and events available for kids. (So alive and well are the arts in Kansas City, that we could have written an entire book on this subject alone!)

As the project grew, so did our enthusiasm. We unearthed child-oriented museums, tours, ethnic dance troupes, entertainers, summer day camps and classes, exhibits and programs showcasing history, nature, science, arts, crafts, sports and more. Plus, we found wonderful experiences for kids and parents to share together.

We're very excited about this book, and we hope that it will prove a useful tool to stimulate the imagination of visitors and residents alike. Most of all, we hope it will provide an entertaining and exciting new way for you and your child to explore Kansas City together.

Shifra Stein

KANSAS CITY AREA MAP

N

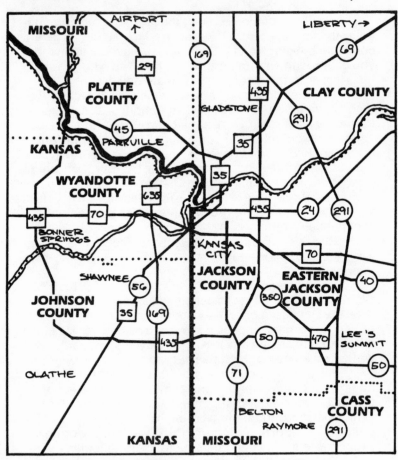

········· COUNTY LINE

▬▬▬▬ STATE LINE

〜〜〜 RIVER

JACKSON COUNTY, MISSOURI

KANSAS CITY, DOWNTOWN, NORTH END, NORTHEAST, WEST, MIDTOWN, SOUTH OF PLAZA, AND EAST OF PLAZA

KEY: (I) individual tours, no reservations needed; (I/R) individual tours, reservations needed; (G) group tours, no reservations needed; (G/R) group tours, reservations needed; ($) fee; (No $) no fee; (B) bathrooms; (No B) no bathrooms; (D) some accommodations for the disabled.

DOWNTOWN (River to 31st St.) NORTH END (River, City Market area), NORTHEAST (9th St. to Cliff Drive, Paseo to Bennington); WEST SIDE (12th St. to 31st St., State Line to S.W. Trafficway)

ASSISTANCE

Convention Bureaus and Chambers of Commerce

Chamber of Commerce of Greater Kansas City, 920 Main St., Kansas City, MO 64105, 221-2424.

Convention and Visitors Bureau of Greater Kansas City, 1100 Main St., Suite 2550, Kansas City, MO 64105, 221-5242. The bureau will send you a map, a list of sights to see, and a book of coupons for hotels and restaurants in the area.

Convention and Visitors Bureau Visitor Information Phone, 471-9600.

Old Northeast Neighborhood Alliance, 532 Benton Blvd., Kansas City, MO 64124, 231-3707.

Clubs and Organizations

Boys and Girls Clubs of Greater Kansas City, 1911 E. 23rd St., Kansas City, MO 64127, 483-4542; 3801 E. 43rd St., Kansas City, MO 64130, 861-6300. The primary focus of the non-profit Boys and Girls Clubs is juvenile delinquency prevention and positive youth development. The agency works with inner city kids to help them gain self-esteem and develop the motivation to become outstanding adults. Counseling, cultural arts, computer education, college work scholarship sessions, teen job placement, learning centers, and sports are part of the program. There's also ongoing support for young people who choose to be drug free. *Time Frame:* After-school to 9 p.m. and all day Saturday. *Ages:* 6 to 17. *Important to Know:* (I) (Small $) (B)

Kansas City, Missouri, Council of Camp Fire. (See Assistance, East of Plaza, Kansas City, MO.)

Heart of America Council, Boy Scouts of America. (See Listing under Assistance, Kansas City, KS.)

The Santa Fe Trail Council of Girl Scouts, Inc. (See Listing under Assistance, Kansas City, KS.)

Mid-Continent Council of Girl Scouts. (See Assistance, East of Plaza.)

YMCA of Greater Kansas City. (See Clubs and Organizations, Midtown Kansas City, MO.)

Special Assistance—Day Care

Division of Family Services, 472-2712, 615 E. 13th St., Kansas City, MO 64106.

YWCA Resource and Referral, 1000 Charlotte, Kansas City, MO 64106, 842-7538. (Listing and providers and centers, by zip code area in Missouri).

Special Assistance for the Disabled

Kansas City Missouri, Parks and Recreation Department. (See Special Assistance for the Disabled, East of Plaza.)

Direction Service Center. (See Listing under Special Assistance for the Disabled, Independence, MO.) This organization publishes a pamphlet featuring summer programs for disabled children.

The Whole Person, Inc. (See Listing under Special Assistance for the Disabled, South of Plaza, Kansas City, MO.) This is a private not-for-profit organization for people with disabilities.

Transportation

The Kansas City Trolley, 707 E. 19th St., P.O. Box 414048, Kansas City, MO 64141, 221-3399. Kids love to ride this trackless trolley that travels between downtown, Westport and the Plaza from March through December.

The Metro, 1350 E. 17th St., Kansas City, MO 64108, 346-0315. Kids under 5 ride free. School children can obtain a half-fare card. Regular passengers can purchase monthly bus passes.

Metropolitan Transportation Services, Inc./Yellow Cab, 505 W. 23rd St., Kansas City, MO 64108, 471-6050. MTSI picks youngsters up at regular times. You can pay the company in advance, so your child doesn't have to deal with money.

Parks and Recreation Departments

Kansas City, Missouri, Parks and Recreation Department, 5605 E. 63rd St., Kansas City, MO 64130, 444-3113. (See Assistance, East of Plaza.)

BUSINESS AND COMMERCIAL TOURS

American Royal, 1701 American Royal Ct., Kansas City, MO 64102, 221-9800. Free school tours are offered during the American Royal in fall. The BOTARS serve as guides for tours of the show animals, arenas and petting zoo. There are special children's performances, and a rodeo and horse show that features acts of special interest to kids. *Time Frame:* 1 hour. *Ages:* pre-school up. *Important to Know:* (G/R) ($ for horse show and rodeo) (B)

City Hall, 414 E. 12th St., Kansas City, MO 64106, 274-2601. Highlights of this tour include a visit to city council chambers, a discussion of city government and a trip to the observation deck. *Time Frame:* 45 minutes. *Ages:* 6 up. *Important to Know:* (I; G/R) (No $) (B) (D)

Federal Courthouse, 811 Grand Ave., Kansas City, MO 64106, 426-2811. This educational opportunity includes a tour of the courthouse. With advance notice, a mock trial can be set up, complete with a real judge and members of the Young Lawyers Association. Children participate in the mock trial as witnesses and jury members. *Time Frame:* about 2 hours. *Ages:* 4th grade up. *Important to Know:* (G/R) (No $) (B)

Federal Reserve Bank, 925 Grand Ave., Kansas City, MO 64198, 881-2200. Parents and children may take self-guided tours of the Visitors Center and the traveling exhibitions in the main floor gallery. The mezzanine level holds interesting hands-on displays of coin and paper money and counterfeit currency. The three-story high lobby usually awes younger kids. The guided group tours for high school age and above include a trip to the cash services and check collection departments, and the vault. *Time Frame:* 30 minutes for the self-guided tours; 75 minutes for group tours. *Ages:* 3 up. *Important to Know:* (No reservations for self-guided tours) (G/R) (No $) (B) (D).

Fire Station #23, 4777 Independence Ave., Kansas City, MO 64124, 231-0445. The tour consists of an informative behind-the-scenes look at the life of a firefighter. Children get a hands-on demonstraton of trucks and equipment and get a lesson on fire prevention and safety. *Time Frame:* 45 minutes. Ages: all. *Important to Know:* (G/R) (No $) (B)

Kansas City, Missouri, Fire Department, 306 E. 12th St., Suite 630, Kansas City, MO 64106, 274-1478. A trip to the fire station comes complete with a tour of firefighter's quarters, alarm office, and rescue equipment. The Fire Department will also send a pumper or ladder truck to schools and groups to provide demonstrations of firefighting skills. *Time Frame:* 45 minutes. *Ages:* all. *Important to Know:* (I/R; G/R) (No $) (B) (D)

Kansas City Public Library, 311 E. 12th St., Kansas City, MO 64106, 221-2685. The main library, like all the branches, offers tours to classes and groups emphasizing library use. *Time Frame:* 45 minutes. *Ages:* K through 6th grade. *Important to Know:* (G/R) (No $) (B) (D)

Green Mill Candy Factory, 2020 Washington, Kansas City, MO 64108, 421-7600. Kids can tour the candy plant and get a taste of assembly line chocolates just like Willy Wonka. At the end of the visit youngsters take home a free bag of peanut brittle and parents get to buy candy at the factory outlet store. *Time Frame:* 45 minutes. *Ages:* all. *Important to know:* (I/R) (G/R) ($) (B)

Hallmark Visitors Center, Hallmark Square at Crown Center, 25th and McGee, Kansas City, MO 64141, 274-5672. The self-guided tour is loaded with colorful hands-on exhibits that highlight the history of Hallmark Cards, Inc. Kids love the giant mug filled with pencils and paints. *Time Frame:* 30 minutes. *Ages:* pre-school up. *Important to Know:* (I/R) (G/R) (No $) (B) (D)

Kansas City Museum Planetarium, 3218 Gladstone Blvd., Kansas City, MO 64123, 483-8300. Choose from several planetarium programs for your tour, all tailored for different ages. Constellations, planets, dinosaurs, and spacecraft are some of the tour possibilities. *Time Frame:* 55 minutes. *Ages:* pre-school through adult. *Important to Know:* (I) (G/R) ($) (B) (D)

KCPT Channel 19 TV Station, 125 E. 31st St., Kansas City, MO 64108, 756-3580. Tours include the offices, studio and engineering/production room. Cameras are turned on the kids at the end so they can see themselves on the monitors. *Time Frame:* 45 minutes. *Ages:* 6-17. *Important to Know:* tours are only as studio schedule allows. (G/R) (No $) (B) (D)

The Metro, 1350 E. 17th St., Kansas City, MO 64108, 346-0315. Children may tour the offices and learn what goes on behind the scenes. They're shown how they can watch for a specific bus and given activity books which teach them how to avoid taking the wrong bus. *Time Frame:* 30 minutes. *Ages:* all. *Important to Know:* (I/R) (G/R) (No $) (B) (D upon advance request)

Starlight Theatre, 4600 Starlight Rd. in Swope Park, **Kansas City, MO 64132, 333-9481.** (See Business and Commercial Tours, East of Plaza.)

U.S. Post Office, 315 W. Pershing Rd., Kansas City, MO 64111, 374-9144. Children learn all the steps of mail processing, from the time they put a letter in the mailbox to the time it's delivered. *Time Frame:* 1 hour. *Ages:* 8 up. *Important to Know:* (G/R) (No $) (B)

The World, 412 Oak St., Kansas City, MO 64106, 474-1794. From desk-top publishing to newspapers "hot off the press," the "World" features an informative tour for kids. They'll see the computers and press room and get a free newspaper at the end of the visit. *Time Frame:* 20 minutes. *Ages:* 4 up. *Important to Know:* small children must be accompanied by a parent. (I/R) (G/R) (No $) (B)

HISTORIC SITES AND MUSEUMS

Black Archives of Mid-America, 2033 Vine, Kansas City, MO 64109, 483-1300. (See Historic Sites and Museums, East of Plaza.)

Thomas Hart Benton Home & Studio, 3616 Belleview, Kansas City, MO 64111, 931-5722. (See Historic Sites and Museums, Midtown.)

Grace and Holy Trinity Cathedral, 13th and Broadway, P.O. 412048, Kansas City, MO 64141, 474-8260. (See The Arts, this section.)

Kansas City Museum, 3218 Gladstone Blvd., Kansas City, MO 64123, 483-8300. (Also see Special Activities and Business and Commercial Tours, this section.) Originally an ornate 70-room mansion, the museum holds fascinating exhibits of frontier life and early regional history. Displays include: replicas of an Osage Indian lodge; a flatboat and covered wagon; native animal dioramas; a planetarium which features a variety of audio/visual presentations; and an old Corner Drugstore that sells old-fashioned sweet treats kids love. Check out the special group tours for children. *Time Frame:* 1 hour. *Ages:* pre-school up. *Important to Know:* (I) (G/R) (No $ with Y.A. Arts Card) (B) (D)

Kansas City Museum, Satellite location, Town Pavilion, 11th and Main, Kansas City, MO 64108, 483-8300. Opened to accommodate popular traveling exhibits, the museum's new 5,700 square foot capability brings Kansas Citians an opportunity to view large-scale shows that have won national acclaim. *Time Frame:* 1 hour. *Ages:* pre-school up. *Important to Know:* (I) (G/R) (donation) (B)

Lewis and Clark Point, 8th and Jefferson Sts., Kansas City, MO. A marker commemorates the spot where the famed explorers camped in 1806. The site overlooks a spectacular view of Kansas City and the Kaw and Missouri Rivers. It's a good way to introduce youngsters to the history of the area. *Time Frame:* up to you. *Ages:* all. *Important to Know:* (I) (G) (No $) (No B)

Liberty Memorial, 100 W. 26th St., Kansas City, MO 64134, 221-1918. This is the only war memorial museum in the country specializing in relics and memorabilia of World War I. Displays of uniforms, insignia and firearms, plus exhibits recreating actual trench conditions with realistic sound effects and lighting are intriguing for kids. Memory Hall contains outstanding paintings and murals. The tower which bears the "Torch of Liberty" is 200 feet tall and has an observation deck at the top. *Time Frame:* 45 minutes. *Ages:* 2nd grade up. *Important to Know:* (I) (G) (No $) (B)

THE ARTS

The arts are abundant in Kansas City and families have a wide variety of possibilities for children. Included here and in other sections of this book are various arts organizations and events suitable for kids.

Young Audiences Arts Card, Kansas City Chapter of Young Audiences™. (See The Arts, Midtown, Kansas City, MO.)

American Heartland Theater, 2450 Grand Ave., Suite 314, Kansas City, MO 64108, 842-9999. Special matinee and student prices. *Important to Know:* ($) (B) (D)

Coterie Children's Theatre, 2450 Grand Ave., Kansas City, MO 64108, 474-6552. This award-winning company's professional performances of original children's plays are held in an intimate Crown Center Theater. Many of the offerings are interpreted for the deaf and hearing-impaired and there is ticket subsidy for economically deprived kids as well. *Ages:* all. *Important to Know:* (I/R) (G/R) ($) (B)

Friends of Chamber Music, P.O. Box 10401, Kansas City, MO 64111, 444-4429. Children-oriented and afternoon family concerts are part of the Friends' programs during the school year. *Time Frame:* 2 hours. *Ages:* 7 up. *Important to Know:* (I/R) (G/R) (free ticket with regular admission ticket with Y.A. Arts Card) (B) (D)

Folly Theater Children's Series, 1029 Central, Kansas City, MO 64106, 474-4444. The Folly offers a children's series on Sundays in January, March, and April featuring visiting troupes of professionals in classic and original plays. They also have a series for schools available through Young Audiences at a modest student fee. *Time Frame:* about 1 hour. *Ages;* 4 to 10. *Important to Know:* (I/R) (G/R) ($) (B) (D) .

Grace and Holy Trinity Cathedral, 415 W. 13th St., P.O. 412048, Kansas City, MO 64141, 474-8260. Boasting the largest mechanical action pipe organ in Missouri, this century-old Cathedral hosts an "Artists Series" which brings in performers from around the world. The concerts, which have showcased artists from England's Westminster Abbey, particularly appeal to youngsters with keyboard experience or those with a keen interest in the musical arts. Kids are invited to tour the cathedral and see the organ with advance notice. *Time Frame:* 1½ hours. *Ages:* 10 up. *Important to Know:* (I) (G) ($) (B) (D)

Kansas City Museum. (See Museums and Historic Sites, this section.)

Kansas City Symphony, 1029 Central, Kansas City, MO 64105, 471-7344. This unstuffy professional orchestra delights in bringing symphonic music and culture to Kansas City kids. Aside from its family-oriented "sampler" concerts, it offers school performances that integrate lectures on music history. Teachers get a manual with tape to discuss the concert with their classes. *Time Frame:* school concerts run 45 minutes. *Ages:* 1st to 8th grade. *Important to Know:* (I/R) (G/R) (No $ for school concerts) (B) (D)

Lyric Opera of Kansas City, 1029 Central, Kansas City, MO 64106, 471-7344. Opera is sung in English in fall and spring seasons. Although most productions are adult-oriented, older children and teenagers might enjoy some performances which provide a surprising alternative to heavy metal rock 'n' roll. *Time Frame:* 2 hours. *Ages:* 11 up. *Important to Know:* (I/R) (G/R) ($) (B) (D)

Midland Center for the Performing Arts, 1228 Main, Kansas City, MO 64105, 421-7500. This gorgeous theater is home for the Theater League which brings national touring companies to town. The season includes Broadway musicals and concerts, many of which appeal to children. *Time Frame:* about 2 hours. *Ages:* 6 up. *Important to Know:* (I/R) (G/R) ($) (B) (D)

Missouri Repertory Theatre. (See The Arts, Midtown)

Nelson-Atkins Museum of Art (See Historic Sites and Museums and The Arts, Midtown.)

Paul Mesner's Puppets, Quality Hill Playhouse, 303 W. 10th St., Kansas City, MO 64105, 421-7500. Nationally reknowned puppeteer, Paul Mesner delights children of all ages with a 4-show series of inventive puppet artistry. The Theater League presentation season runs from September to May. *Time Frame:* 1 hour. *Ages:* 6 to 12. *Important to Know:* (I/R) (G/R) ($) (B) (D)

Starlight Theater, 4600 Starlight Rd., Kansas City, MO 64132, 333-9481. (See The Arts, East of Plaza.)

State Ballet of Missouri (See The Arts, Midtown.)

Summer Youth Enrichment Program, 444 St. John Ave., Kansas City, MO 64123, 231-4443. Area community center children can audition for "A Children's Musical," held annually at the Kansas City Music Hall at 13th and Wyandotte. The audition involves singing and dancing. If the youngsters are accepted, there's a 5-week rehearsal period to sharpen their skills. *Ages:* 6 to 13. *Important to Know:* (I/R) (No $) (B)

Theater Under the Stars, 31st and Pennsylvania (Penn Valley Community College), Kansas City, MO 64111, 444-3113. This Parks and Recreation-sponsored community theater performs family-oriented musicals. *Time Frame:* about 1½ hours. *Ages:* 5 up. *Important to Know:* (I) (G) (No $) (B)

Theatre for Young America (See The Arts, Overland Park, KS.)

Westport Ballet (See The Arts, Midtown.)

The William Jewell College Fine Arts Program (See The Arts, Liberty, MO.)

Young Audiences, 4510 Belleview, Suite 116, Kansas City, MO 64111, 531-4022. (See The Arts, Midtown.)

AMUSEMENTS

Crown Center Ice Terrace, 2450 Grand, Kansas City, MO 64108, 474-4400. Open in winter, the ice terrace is a fun place for kids and parents who can join their youngsters and glide along, taking their share of spills. Skating classes are offered. *Ages:* K up. *Important to Know:* (I) (G) ($) (B)

Worlds of Fun, 4545 Worlds of Fun Avenue, Kansas City, MO 64161, 454-4444. (See Worlds of Fun and Oceans of Fun listings under Amusements, Clay County.)

SPORTS

Allen's Bowl, 4835 Independence Blvd., Kansas City, MO 64124, 483-6666. This is a favorite spot for Northeast families. Close to a bus stop, it features lessons and special leagues for kids. *Ages:* 5 up. *Important to Know:* (I) (G/R) ($) (B) (D)

Comets Soccer, Kemper Arena, 1800 Genessee, Kansas City, MO 64102, 421-6460. This Major Indoor Soccer League plays home games at Kemper Arena from November through April. Children 12 years and under get half-price tickets. (I/R) (G/R) ($) (B) (D)

Guadalupe Center, Inc., 2641 Belleview, Kansas City, MO 64108, 561-6885, 472-5108. Year-around recreational team sports are offered evenings and weekends for boys and girls and include baseball, softball, basketball and more. *Ages:* K through high school. *Important to Know:* (I/R) (No $) (B)

PLAYING TOGETHER

Northeast Moms and Tots, 141 S. Van Brunt Blvd.,
Kansas City, MO 64124, 231-4138, 231-6236. This support
group provides a wide range of activities for moms and kids
including field trips, special events, and holiday season
projects where everyone participates. Guest speakers are
invited each month to discuss topics of interest. *Ages:*
newborn to 6. *Important to Know:* (I) ($)

Northeast Library PACT (Parents and Children Together),
6000 Wilson Rd., Kansas City, MO 64123, 231-6313. This
reading program encourages kids and parents to share
special reading time together. A total of 20 books read by
parents to children nets a free paperback; 200 books garners
a pin. It's a great way for kids to develop a love and understanding of books. *Ages:* pre-schoolers. *Important to Know:*
(I) (No $) (D)

Parents as Teachers, 1211 McGee, Rm. 807, Kansas City,
MO 64106, 374-0413. This pilot program of the Kansas City,
MO School District features private visits with parent-
educators as well as group meetings with other parents.
There's a toy lending library and resource center, as well as
vision, hearing, and physical development evaluation test-
ing for kids. Parents can take advantage of the children's
learning opportunities to teach their kids. *Ages:* infant to 3.
Important to Know: (No $)

THE GREAT OUTDOORS

Kansas City, Missouri, Parks and Recreation
Department, 5605 E. 63rd St., Kansas City, MO 64130, 444-
3113. (See Assistance, East of Plaza.)

Special Area Parks and Playgrounds

Most area parks offer picnic areas, ball fields, tennis courts,
playgrounds, shelters and more. Included are a few play-
grounds with drop-in program activities that include arts,

crafts, and games. Most have bathrooms. Phone the Kansas City, MO Parks and Recreation Department for information. (See Assistance, East of Plaza.) In the meantime, this is a sampling of what you'll find:

Budd Park, St. John and Hardesty. Has a pool and walking trail.

Concourse Park (The Park of Fountains), Benton Blvd. and Gladstone Blvd. Many seasonal events take place here including the annual Italian Festival and Easter Parade. In winter the fountains create a lovely ice sculpture.

Indian Mound, Gladstone Blvd. and Belmont. This park/playground has an interesting history. Indian remains have been found in and around here. Across from the park, an observation point overlooks the cliffs.

Kessler Park, Gladstone Blvd. and 32nd St., across from The Kansas City Museum. This is where many special events are held. Entertainers perform here in summer. Kite-flying and sledding are popular activities.

Terrace Lake/Cliff Drive, Gladstone Blvd. and Cliff Drive. In its heyday Cliff Drive was one of the best scenic views in the city. New measures have been taken to keep Cliff Drive safe. Security guards and street lights have been added and renovation includes a newly reconstructed lake that offers fishing and swimming as well as biking and hiking trails that surround the area. Kite festivals, 10 K runs, and a waterfall bring in visitors throughout the year to this lovely area. Access to Cliff Drive is just east of the Kansas City Museum off of Gladstone Blvd.

Summer Camping Programs

Summer Daze, Kansas City, Missouri, Parks and Recreation Department, 5605 E. 63rd St., Kansas City, MO 64130, 444-3113. The program features a week of athletics and tournaments. At the end of that time, there's a play day in the park with magicians, mimes and clowns. This gives youngsters a chance to get some exercise along with their fun.

Ages: 5 to 16. *Important to Know:* this program is a lifesaver for parents who've got bored kids sitting around in the summer heat. Free transportation is provided. (No $)

Guadalupe Center, Inc., 2641 Belleview, **Kansas City, MO 64108, 561-6885, 472-5108.** The center features summer day camps for children at their educational building, Plaza de Ninos. *Ages:* 6 to 13. *Important to Know:* ($) (B)

Whatsoever Circle Community House, 1201 Ewing, **Kansas City, MO 64126, 231-0227.** (See Special Activities, this section.)

SPECIAL LIBRARY PROGRAMS

Northeast Library PACT (Parents and Children Together), **5902 Wilson Rd., Kansas City, MO 64123, 231-6313.** (See Playing Together, Downtown.)

Special Programs, Kansas City Public Library, 311 **E. 12th St., Kansas City, MO 64106, 221-2685, ext. 131.** The main library offers an 8-week summer program featuring classes in cartooning, crafts and celebrations. The library also features films for children and a summer reading program with incentives, plus a pre-school story hour and "Dial-A-Story," where children can listen to a favorite tale on the phone by calling 842-BOOK. Phone the main library for information about branch library activities in your area. *Ages:* 3 to 12. *Important to Know:* (I) (G) (No $) (B)

ENTERTAINING PEOPLE

Ross Balano, 3628 Gladstone Blvd., **Kansas City, MO 64123, 231-3584.** This magician offers everything from close-up magic to the largest of illusions. His saw-the-woman-in-half routine can be performed for special parties. Children can participate by helping with some of the tricks. *Ages:* all. *Important to Know:* (I/R) (G/R) ($)

El Grupos Atotonilco, 2641 Belleview, Kansas City, MO 64108, 561-6885. This group of children, selected from area communities, is available to entertain at parties and other functions with their interpretations of Mexican Folklore Dances. (G/R) (No $)

SPECIAL ACTIVITIES

City Market, Main and 5th Sts., Kansas City, MO 64106. Bustling Saturday mornings are fun for families who come to see and buy everything from farm-fresh produce to crafts and live animals. It's a must for those kids who think food automatically comes wrapped in plastic. *Ages:* all. *Important to Know:* (B) (D)

Don Bosco Community Center, 526 Campbell, Kansas City, MO 64106, 221-6122. Equipped with a gym and game room, the center offers field trips, special activities and events for youngsters. *Ages:* 6 up. *Important to Know:* (I/R) (G/R) ($ for some activities) (B)

Guadalupe Center, Inc., 2641 Belleview, Kansas City, MO 64108, 561-6885, 472-5108. The center's bilingual pre-school features an English/Spanish curriculum for students. After-school and school supplement programs for children ages K through 5th grade feature reading, math, computer introduction, and science classes. There are reading improvement courses for 7th to 9th graders as well as after-school latchkey programs for youngsters K through 8th grade. Tutorials in math, English and job skills for "at risk and dropout" youth are also part of the center's educational focus. *Important to Know:* all ethnic backgrounds welcome. (I/R) ($) (B)

Heart of America Family Services, 3217 Broadway, Suite 500, Kansas City, MO 64111, 753-5280. This agency features a bundle of programs and activities for kids and parents designed to improve parent-child relationships as well as self-esteem and social skills. "PhoneFriend," a telephone reassurance program, is designed for latchkey kids who can call if they are lonely, scared or need a grown-up to reassure them. The organization also has a large selection of informative family-oriented films and cassettes available for a nominal rental fee. *Ages:* 5 up. *Important to Know:* ($ based on ability to pay) (B)

Kaleidoscope, P.O. Box 419580, 25th and McGee, Crown Center, Kansas City, MO 64141, 274-8301. A Hallmark original, Kaleidoscope offers children a total experience in which they use all their senses. After a tour through the playroom, youngsters can visit various arts and crafts project tables and make gifts to take home. Parents are not allowed in, but they may watch through one-way mirrors. The kids have a ball! *Time Frame:* 1½ hours. *Ages:* 5 to 12. *Important to Know:* (I/R) (G/R) ($) (B) (D)

KPL Gas Service Company, 2460 Pershing Rd., Kansas City, MO 64108, 221-4765. The company's Safety Watch program for youngsters features the "Take a Bite Out of Crime" logo on the company vehicles. Kids who are lost or in trouble can come to the truck for help. KPL also donates safety coloring books to classrooms to acquaint students and teachers with the program. *Ages:* 5 to 10. *Important to Know:* (G/R) (No $)

Kansas City, Missouri, Fire Department, 306 E. 12th St., Suite 630, Kansas City, MO 64106, 274-1478. (Also see Business and Commercial Tours, Kansas City, MO.) The Fire Department comes to schools and groups and puts on fire safety programs which include a talking fire hydrant, and information on fire prevention and survival. *Ages:* all. *Important to Know:* (G/R) (No $)

Kansas City, Missouri, Parks and Recreation Community Centers, 274-1671. Arts and crafts, sports and fishing are offered by the following Kansas City, Missouri Parks and Recreation Community Centers as part of their summer activities for children:

Blue Valley Recreation Center, 18th and White, 241-6491.

Garrison Community Center, 1123 E. 5th St., 274-1538.

Gregg Community Center, 1600 E. 17th Terr., 274-1698.

The Learning Exchange, 2720 Walnut, Kansas City, MO 64108, 234-9184. Children can create their own presents to give for special occasions at the Kids' Workshop where they'll find plenty of arts and crafts makings for a modest fee. Adult supervision is necessary. Fifth graders can also take school field trips to Exchange City, a model city where they'll learn about business and finance. *Ages:* Kids' Workshop: pre-schoolers up. *Important to Know:* (I/R) (G/R) ($) (B) (D)

Northeast Owl Center, 4444 St. John Ave., Kansas City, MO 64123, 231-4443. The center's summer recreation program for kids consists of arts and crafts, swimming, soccer and more. Tutors are provided for children ages 3 to 8. Dance and music sessions are held in fall and winter. *Ages:* 6 to 16. *Important to Know:* (I/R) ($) (B)

Starlab Portable Planetarium, Kansas City Museum, 3218 Gladstone Blvd., Kansas City, MO 64123, 483-8300. (Also see Museums and Historic Sites, Kansas City, MO.) This portable, inflatable planetarium accommodates groups of elementary and high school students. There are several programs from which to choose including galaxies, constellations, and a visit inside a biological cell. *Time Frame:* 45 minutes. *Ages:* K to adult. *Important to Know:* (G/R) ($)

Stockyards Livestock Exchange, 1600 Genessee, Kansas City, MO 64102, 842-6800. Visitors are welcome to attend the cattle auctions on Wednesday and Thursday mornings. While you're not allowed into the stockyards, themselves, you can still walk around the outside to see the animals. *Ages:* 1st grade up. *Important to Know:* (I) (G) (No $) (B)

Sunday Night Concert Series, Kansas City, Missouri, Parks and Recreation Department, 5605 E. 63rd St., Kansas City, MO 64130, 444-3113. The department offers free concerts throughout the summer for families. Bring a picnic supper for the kids. *Time Frame:* about 2 hours. *Ages:* all. *Important to Know:* (I) (G) (No $) (No B)

Summer on the Square Concerts, Crown Center Square, 2450 Grand, Kansas City, MO 64108, 474-4400.

Fridays in summer Crown Center is the place to come for top-name musicians and free outdoor concerts. You can wander around the fountains and outdoor food kiosks while you listen. *Time Frame:* about 2 hours. *Ages:* 10 up enjoy it the most. *Important to Know:* (I) (G) (No $) (B)

Whatsoever Circle Community House, 1201 Ewing, Kansas City, MO 64126, 231-0227. A summer day camp for youngsters ages 4 to 13 is offered complete with athletic programs, a gym, movies and entertainment, kids clubs, and game room. There is a free well baby clinic for special health needs, plus a monthly family night for parents and children. *Ages:* pre-school up. *Important to Know:* (I/R) (G/R) ($ for some activities) (B)

Zoobilee Zoo, P.O. Box 8536KC, Lincoln, NE 68544. Kansas City is the birthplace of this rollicking Hallmark Properties live-action television show for kids. They can join the Zoobilee Zoo Fan Club and, as members, receive a letter from their favorite Zooble, and a newsletter crammed with activities, gifts and more. *Ages:* all. *Important to Know:* (I) ($)

SPECIAL EVENTS CALENDAR

FEBRUARY

N.A.I.A. Track and Field Championship, Municipal Auditorium, 1221 Baltimore, Kansas City, MO 64105. (NOTE: Location, times, and dates vary.) Hundreds of top athletes from the National Association of Intercollegiate Athletics compete in this event. *Important to Know:* ($) (D)

MARCH

Big 8 Conference Basketball Tournament, 600 E. 8th St., Kansas City, MO 64106, 471-5088. (NOTE: Location, times, and dates vary.) The conference serves eight universities in intercollegiate athletics. Kansas City plays host for some games. *Important to Know:* ($) (D)

N.A.I.A. National Basketball Tournament, 1221 Baltimore, Kansas City, MO 64105, 842-5050. (NOTE: Location, times, and dates vary.) This organization provides various colleges with an intercollegiate athletic program. Both men and women participate. *Important to Know:* ($) (D)

St. Patrick's Day Parade, Pershing and Main. Each year the parade winds its way downtown on St. Patrick's Day to the delight of onlookers who like watching the kaleidoscopic display of floats and participants. *Important to Know:* (No $)

APRIL

Concours d'Elegance, Associated Car Clubs of Kansas City, Kansas City Museum grounds, 3218 Gladstone Blvd., Kansas City, MO 64123, 483-8300. This annual invitational exhibition of antique and classic cars has over 100 rare autos on display to delight kids of all ages. The event features a photography contest with prizes for the best color and black and white shots taken by youngsters 18 and under. *Important to Know:* ($)

Ice Capades, Kemper Arena, 1800 Genessee, Kansas City, MO 64102, 421-6460. This family favorite is always a winner for kids. Highlights are audience participation, colorful costumes and spectacular skating. *Important to Know:* ($)

MAY

Missouri Reservoir Kite Festival, Northeast Area Merchants Assn., 100 Wabash in Cliff Drive, Kansas City, MO 64124, 241-2288. All Kansas City residents are welcome to participate in the kite-flying. Kids receive free food, drink, music and toy surprises including a kite. *Important to Know:* (No $)

JUNE

Ethnic Heritage Performances, Kansas City, Missouri, Parks and Recreation Department, 5605 E. 63rd St., Kansas City, MO 64130, 444-3113. The department brings ethnic performers onstage at locations around the city to bring their musical heritage to Kansas Citians. The shows can be very exciting to children and stimulate interest in other cultures. *Important to Know:* (No $)

JULY

Double Dutch Competition, Gregg Community Center, 1600 E. 17th Terr., Kansas City, MO 64108, 274-1698, 444-9080. This annual rope-jumping competition for boys and girls ages 15 and under features teams of rope turners and jumpers who compete for prizes in skill, speed and showmanship. *Important to Know:* (No $)

SEPTEMBER

Heart of America Quilt Show, The Greater Kansas City Quilters Guild, Crown Center Shops Exhibition Hall, Kansas City, MO 64108. Colorful quilts are displayed and sold to raise money for the Mayor's Christmas Tree Fund. Many of the designs are whimsical enough to delight children. *Important to Know:* (No $ to look)

Hispanic Ethnic Week, Guadalupe Center, Inc., 2641 Belleview, Kansas City, MO 64108, 561-6885. Barney Allis Plaza is the site for this colorful festival which features booths with traditional Hispanic dishes and entertainment. *Important to Know:* (No $)

Kansas City Spirit Festival. Location, time, and dates may vary. 221-4444. Local and national entertainment, food, music and more are part of the Spirit Festival. There are plenty of activities for kids culminating in a gigantic fireworks display to liven their interest. *Important to Know:* ($) (D)

Labor Day Weekend at Crown Center, Westin Crown Center Hotel, One Pershing Rd., Kansas City, MO 64108, 474-4400, Ext. 2217. Each Labor Day the Jerry Lewis Muscular Dystrophy Telethon raises money for MDA. Families can come and take part in the 24-hour live broadcast from the hotel lobby. Before the telethon, there's a "bed race" where colorfully costumed teams race specially designed beds down the streets surrounding the hotel. It's silly, but kids love it. *Important to Know:* (No $)

OCTOBER

Cliffhanger Run, Northeast World, 412 Oak, Kansas City, MO 64106, 474-1794. The 10 K, 5 K, and 2 mile runs are held in conjunction with the Italian Festival and proceeds benefit a different hot-for-profit organization each year. Aside from the fun, the northeast cliffs provide a scenic route for the run and, at the culminating point, kids are met by clowns, magicians and pony rides. *Important to Know:* ($)

Festa Italia (Italian Festival), Concourse Park, Benton Blvd. and Gladstone Blvd., Kansas City, MO 64127. Held around Columbus Day, the 3-day event provides plenty of authentic Italian food and lots of activities including entertainment by magicians, singers, and comedians. Kids love the games, clowns, mimes and pony rides. *Important to Know:* (No $)

Kansas City Chocolate Plus Festival, Friends of the Lyric Opera, mailing address, 10305 Wenonga Rd., S.M., KS 66206, 341-2633. This chocoholics dream-come-true features a mind-boggling variety of candy and pastries that youngsters love. Many of the artistic creations by area chefs and candymakers amaze the eye as well as tempt the palate. *Important to Know:* ($)

Snoopy's Pumpkin Patch, Crown Center Square, 2450 Grand, Kansas City, MO 64108, 274-4444. Snoopy hosts this Halloween event that benefits UNICEF. For $1 donation, kids can select their own pumpkin from the patch and decorate it on the spot. There's entertainment, a carnival and games to go along with the fun. *Important to Know:* ($ donation)

NOVEMBER

American Royal Livestock, Horse Show and Rodeo, 1701 American Royal Ct., Kansas City, MO 64102, 221-9800. Since 1899 the nation's largest combined livestock show and rodeo has attracted competitors from around the country who take part in one of Kansas City's most famous traditions. Also featured is a grand parade, western show, and barbecue contest. *Important to Know:* ($) (D)

DECEMBER

The Mayor's Christmas Tree Lighting Ceremony, Crown Center Square, 2450 Grand, Kansas City, MO 64108, 474-4400. The Friday after Thanksgiving the lighting ceremony kicks off the campaign to raise money for needy persons in the area. People turn out to hear Christmas carols sung by the Crown Center All-Metro Student Choir and watch as characters from the popular kids' show, Zoobilee Zoo, help the mayor light the tree. *Important to Know:* (No $)

Christmas at Crown Center, The Westin Crown Center Hotel, One Pershing Rd., Kansas City, MO 64108, 474-4400, Ext. 2217. At Christmas the lobby of the hotel is filled with antique and historical Santa Clauses displayed with placards explaining their derivations and significance. The Santas share the spotlight with a fairyland of sugar castles and churches. *Important to Know:* (No $)

Holiday Memories, The Kansas City Museum, 3218 Gladstone Blvd., Kansas City, MO 64123, 483-8300. The traditional Christmas Fairy Princess, formerly displayed at downtown's old Kline's Department Store, is recreated authentically at the museum. Kids can whisper a Christmas wish to the white-gowned Princess and, in return, they receive a special gift magically presented by her. ***Important to Know:*** ($) (D)

FUN EATS

Space limitations prevented us from listing some of the finer dining establishments that cater to families. However we wanted to include just a few quick-stop spots for parents on the go with kids in tow.

Chubby's Breakfast and Burgers, 1835 Independence Ave., Kansas City, MO 64124, 842-2482. Take the kids back in time to this 1950's-style restaurant that serves the good old-fashioned burgers, "curly q" French fries, and ice-cream sodas. Youngsters get free lollipops to take home. (D)

Hav-A-Snack, 2641 Van Brunt, Kansas City, MO 64128, 924-1787. A favorite neighborhood hang-out for lunch and after-school get-togethers, this is where junior high and high school kids come for Italian steak and sausage sandwiches along with cheeseburgers, fries and other fast foods.

Fast Food Havens, 4800 Block through the 600 Block of Independence Ave. Pizza, burgers, fried chicken and tacos are part of the fare you'll find here.

GOODIES

The Candy Barrel, Level One, Crown Center Shops, 2450 Grand, Kansas City, MO 64108, 842-0606. The shop sells candy by the pound from around the world.

The 1910 Corner Drugstore, Kansas City Museum, 3218 Gladstone Blvd., Kansas City, MO 64123, 483-8300. After a tour through the museum, head downstairs to visit this authentic, restored drugstore furnished with a soda fountain that sells old-fashioned sodas, phosphates, and sundaes. Kids love the atmosphere and the tasty treats. (D)

Dari Dip 'N' Deli, 5216 Independence Ave., Kansas City, MO 64123, 483-9899. A variety of ice cream and sodas, fresh donuts made daily, plus hot salami, provolone and Italian meatball sandwiches are served in an old ice cream store ambiance. There are novelty treats for kids including flavored popcorn. (D)

Green Mill Candy Factory, 2020 Washington, Kansas City, MO 64108, 421-7600. (See Business and Commercial Tours, Kansas City, MO.)

Kansas City Fudge, Level One, Crown Center Shops, 2450 Grand, Kansas City, MO 64108, 421-0012. Kids like watching the fudge being made before their eyes. Huge dippers pour forth the gooey brown stuff onto a marble cooling table where it's cut into slabs.

ASSISTANCE

Clubs and Organizations

Boys and Girls Clubs of Greater Kansas City, 1911
**E. 23rd St., Kansas City, MO 64127, 483-4542; 3801 E. 43rd
St., Kansas City, MO 64130, 861-6300.** (See Assistance,
Downtown Kansas City, MO.)

YMCA of Greater Kansas City, 3100 Broadway, Suite
930, Kansas City, MO 64111, 561-9622. The YMCA has an
abundance of sports and cultural programs for kids, plus
day camps, child care, and other offerings. Rather than
trying to list them all in our limited space, we suggest calling
the main YMCA number above for information on the YMCA
location nearest you. (D)

BUSINESS AND COMMERCIAL TOURS

Battle of Westport Tour, Westport Historical Society,
4000 Baltimore, Kansas City, MO 64111, 561-1821. The Battle
of Westport took place in 1864 and was a major Civil War
confrontation. There are 25 descriptive markers at key battle
sites and the self-guided drive/walk tour covers 32 miles
across Kansas City. The society provides a free map and
detailed directions. *Time Frame:* an afternoon. *Ages:* 9 up.
Important to Know: This educational family outing needs
some preparation. Read about the battle before you tour, so
history can really come alive to imaginative youngsters.
(No $) (No B)

Board of Trade, 4800 Main, Kansas City, MO 64110, 753-
7500. One of the country's largest commodities and futures
exchanges, the Board of Trade provides weekly tours that
feature a glimpse of the bustling activity on the trading room
floor. Guides provide plenty of information about what goes
on here. There is also an audio/visual presentation that may

interest older children. *Time Frame:* about an hour. *Ages:* 2nd grade up. *Important to Know:* (I/R) (G/R) (No $) (B)

Nelson-Atkins Museum School Tours. 4525 Oak, **Kansas City, MO 64111, 561-4000, Ext. 238, 931-4278.** The museum has 14 different tours for school and other youth groups. Subjects include everything from African Art and Storytelling to early American pioneer and Indian life. *Time Frame:* 1 hour. *Ages;* 6 through teens. *Important to Know:* the gallery requires one adult for every 10 children. (G/R) (No $) (B)

HISTORIC SITES AND MUSEUMS

Creative Arts Center, Nelson-Atkins Museum of Art, 4525 **Oak St., Kansas City, MO 64111, 931-4278.** (Also see Playing Together.) The Center offers studio classrooms where children can experiment creatively with different media and learn about art from professional educators. *Time Frame:* 1½ hours. *Ages:* 3 to 16. *Important to Know:* (I/R) (G/R) ($) (B)

The Harris-Kearney House, 4000 Baltimore, Kansas **City, MO 64111, 561-1821.** Built in 1855 by John Harris, this museum was once a hotel famed throughout the old West for its hospitality and food. Now the location of the Westport Historical Society as well as being listed on the National Register of Historic Places, the house is open to tour. Children can see authentically furnished rooms and learn about early Kansas City history. *Time Frame:* less than 1 hour. *Ages:* 9 up. *Important to Know:* take your own historic tour of the area by picking up a free pamphlet and map here that shows the location of Westport's old homes. (I) (G/R) ($) (B)

Nelson-Atkins Museum of Art, 4525 Oak St., Kansas **City, MO 64111, 561-4000.** One of the country's top art museums, the Nelson is full of fascinating displays for youngsters including African, Indian, Oriental and contemporary art. Downstairs, the Creative Arts Center holds work by children on display. If you get hungry, Rozzelle Court features excellent cuisine. Guided tours are available. *Time Frame:* up to you. *Ages:* pre-school up. *Important to Know:* (I) (G/R) (free admission with Y.A. Arts Card) (B)

Thomas Hart Benton Home & Studio, 3616 Belleview, Kansas City, MO 64111, 931-5722. Guides take you through the famed Missouri artist's home where he spent the last part of his life. His studio is set up as it was when he used it. Children can view the artist's work and listen to highlights of Benton's colorful years. *Time Frame:* 45 minutes. *Ages:* 5-17. *Important to Know:* (I) (G/R) ($) (B)

Wagonmaster Statue, at the Ward Pkwy. entrance of the new Ritz-Carlton Hotel, Wornall Rd. at Ward Pkwy. Press the button located at the base of the statue and listen to the taped narration about the historic Civil War encounter fought on high ground overlooking what is now the Country Club Plaza. This is where 20,000 Union soldiers finally overcame the tired, ragged Confederates. If there's time, drive from here to the tree-shaded Confederate Memorial at 55th and Ward Parkway. Children may be interested in seeing these rare reminders of the turmoil that occurred here. *Important to Know:* (I) (G) (No $) (No B)

John Wornall House, 146 W. 61st Terr., Kansas City, MO 64113, 444-1858. This 1858 home was used as a field hospital during the Civil War's Battle of Westport. A tour provides insights into the lives of Missouri settlers. Check out activities for children in summer and winter, including nature study, Indian crafts, bread-baking and other aspects of pre-Civil-war life. *Time Frame:* 30 minutes. *Ages:* 3 up. *Important to Know:* (I) (G/R) ($) (B)

THE ARTS

Mattie Rhodes Counseling and Art Center, 915 W. 17th St., Kansas City, MO 64108, 221-2349. The center deals in visual arts and crafts for children. Programs include pottery, woodwork, mask-making and more. Youngsters learn how to work with their hands and are motivated to express themselves. *Time Frame:* 30 minutes. *Ages:* 5 to 12. *Important to Know:* (I) ($) (B)

Missouri Repertory Theater, 4949 Cherry, Performing Arts Center, Kansas City, MO 64110, 276-2727. The "Rep" is reknowned for fine, innovative theater. Although most performances are more suitable for adults and teens, the company has offerings that appeal to kids including "Alice in Wonderland," and the seasonal "A Christmas Carol" which is signed for hearing-impaired. *Time Frame:* about 2 hours. *Ages:* 5 up. *Important to Know:* (I/R) (G/R) (half off admission price with the Y.A. Arts Card) (B) (D)

Nelson-Atkins Museum of Art, 4525 Oak St., Kansas City, MO 64111, 561-4000 (See Historic Sites and Museums, this section.)

State Ballet of Missouri, 706 W. 42nd St., Kansas City, MO 64111, 931-2232. The only fully professional ballet company in Missouri, the State Ballet performs classical and contemporary works with some performances, such as "The Nutcracker," of particular interest to children. *Time Frame:* about 1½ hours. *Ages:* 7 up. *Important to Know:* (I/R) (G/R) (half off admission with Y.A. Arts Card) (B)

UMKC Conservatory of Music, 4420 Warwick, Kansas City, MO 64110, 276-2741. The conservatory provides professional musical training to students seeking music degrees. It also provides music classes for children in a wide variety of instruments and in voice and theory. Suzuki classes in flute and violin are also available. There are regular recitals. *Ages:* 3 up. *Important to Know:* (I/G) (G/R) ($) (B)

Westport Ballet, 3936 Main, Kansas City, MO 64111, 531-4330. Part of the Folly Theatre Children's Series, the Ballet offers eight spring performances specifically designed for children, such as "Hansel and Gretel," "Wizard of Oz," and others. *Time Frame:* 1 hour. *Ages:* 4 up. *Important to Know:* (I/R) (G/R) ($) (B) (D)

Young Audiences Arts Card, Kansas City Chapter of Young Audiences,™ 4510 Belleview, Kansas City, MO 64111, 531-4022. The Arts Card is an absolute must for families who want to expose their children to cultural events. Students grades K-12 receive free or half off admission prices for many major arts and cultural experiences by using the Young Audiences Arts Card. There is no charge for the card and it's a great way to introduce kids to ballet, theater, museums, and musical events.

Young Audiences, 4510 Belleview, Kansas City, MO 64111, 531-4022. Young Audiences works with school districts to expose students to arts organizations in the metro area. School-based activities include lectures, classroom workshops, and artist-in-residence programs. With the free Y.A. Arts Card, kids get discounts on major arts programs.

Youth Symphony of Kansas City, 7645 Tomahawk, Prairie Village, KS 66208, 642-7141. This student orchestra is committed to public performances of classical music. Children who are talented and interested in music may like being part of the orchestra and/or attending yearly concerts performed by their peers. *Time Frame:* 45-75 minutes. *Ages:* 10 to 21. *Important to Know:* (I/R) (G/R) ($) (B) (D)

SPORTS

Kansas City Track Club, 620 W. 26th St., Kansas City, MO 64108, 471-KCTC. Comprised of runners of all ages, the club holds road races, potluck running events at members' homes, and more. By combining the sport of running with social activities, youngsters can make friends with others who have similar interests. Parents can sprint with their kids and join them at social gatherings. Running with a group also affords the added benefit of companionship and safety. *Ages:* 11 to adult. *Important to Know:* (I) (G) ($)

PLAYING TOGETHER

Nelson-Atkins Museum of Art Creative Arts Center, 4525 Oak, Kansas City, MO 64111, 561-4000, Ext. 236. Does your child have an interest in art? Here's the place for you to find out. The center provides arts programs all year for parents and children who want to experiment creatively together in a studio workshop setting and learn to look at art through guided museum walks. *Time Frame:* 1 hour. *Ages:* 3 to 6. *Important to Know;* (I/R) ($) (B)

Kansas City Track Club, 620 W. 26th St., Kansas City, MO 64108, 471-KCTC. (See Sports, Midtown.)

THE GREAT OUTDOORS

Kansas City, Missouri, Parks and Recreation Department, 5605 E. 63rd St., Kansas City, MO 64130, 444-3113. (See Assistance, East of Plaza.)

Special Programs and Exhibits

Sunday Night Concert Series, Kansas City, Missouri, Parks and Recreation Department, 5605 E. 63rd St., Kansas City, MO 64130, 444-3113. These free concerts, given in parks around the city, bring in big-name performers. Bring a picnic basket and the kids.

Special Area Parks and Playgrounds

Most area parks offer picnic areas, ball fields, tennis courts, playgrounds, shelters and more. A few playgrounds have drop-in program activities that include arts, crafts, and games. Most have bathrooms. Phone the Kansas City, MO,

Parks and Recreation Department for information. (See Assistance, East of Plaza.) In the meantime, here are a couple of midtown locations:

Gillham Park, 41st St. and Gillham Rd.

Swinney School, 1106 W. 47th St.

SPECIAL LIBRARY PROGRAMS

Plaza Library, 4801 Main, Kansas City, MO 64111, 753-6114. The Plaza library offers a summer program featuring folksingers, clowns, craft programs, story hours, computer software games, special films and book club with incentives for children. Special holiday events are also scheduled. *Ages:* 3 to 12. *Important to Know:* (I) (G/R) (No $) (B) (D)

SPECIAL ACTIVITIES

Westport Roanoke Community Center, 3601 Roanoke Rd., Kansas City, MO 64111, 531-4106. The Parks and Recreation-sponsored center has after-school activities that include dance and tumbling classes, music lessons, game room, gymnastics and more. *Ages:* 3 to 15. *Important to Know:* ($) (B)

Board of Trade, 4800 Main, Kansas City, MO 64110, 753-7500. (Also see Business and Commercial Tours, Midtown). No reservations are needed to view trading-floor activity of one of the country's largest commodities and futures exchanges. Tours need to be booked in advance. *Time Frame:* about 15 minutes. *Ages:* 2nd grade up. *Important to Know:* (I) (No $) (B)

SPECIAL EVENTS CALENDAR

APRIL

Plaza Easter Parade and Egg Hunt, The Plaza Merchants Assn., 4625 Wornall Rd., Kansas City, MO 64112, 753-

0100. Every Easter, Kansas Citians dress in their spring finery and participate in the annual Easter Parade. The fun includes an Easter Egg Hunt for kids, with contests and prizes. *Important to Know:* (No $)

MAY

Radio Day, Kansas City Symphony and Kansas City Radio Stations, Nelson Gallery Grounds, Brush Creek Blvd. and Oak St., Kansas City, MO 64111, 471-7344. Bring the family and a picnic supper and come enjoy this entertaining evening of classical and Broadway music. *Important to Know:* (No $)

SEPTEMBER

Plaza Art Fair, The Plaza Merchants Assn., 4625 Wornall Rd., Kansas City, MO 64112, 753-0100. This popular outdoor art fair brings in artists from around the country who display their work to thousands of visitors each year. Children like the bustle, the colorful displays and the street food. (No $)

OCTOBER

"Scarey Sunday," Nelson-Atkins Museum of Art, 4525 Oak, Kansas City, MO 64111, 561-4000, Ext. 236. The weekend before Halloween, kids can dress up in their scariest costumes and visit the Nelson where they'll be treated to movies, storytellers, and more. They'll get to decorate their own trick or treat sacks to take home. *Ages:* all. *Important to Know:* (I) (G) (No $) (B) (D)

NOVEMBER

Plaza Lighting Ceremony, The Plaza Merchants Assn., 4625 Wornall Rd., Kansas City, MO 64112, 753-0100. Each Thanksgiving, thousands of people flock to the Plaza to watch the mayor throw the switch that illuminates the famous Plaza Christmas lights. Kids love watching the Country Club Plaza turn a fantasyland ablaze with color. (No $)

FUN EATS

Winsteads, 101 Brush Creek, Kansas City, MO 64112, 753-2244. Winstead's has several locations around the city, but this is the original, complete with triple cheeseburgers, frosty malts, skyscraper sodas, and delectable onion rings. (D)

GOODIES

Hall's Candies, 211 Nichols Rd., Kansas City, MO 64111, 274-3470. (Also see Crown Center location.) Foot-long sticks of bubble gum, chocolates in "crayola" wrappers, and jelly bellies are just part of the kid-pleasing assortment found here.

Lamar's Donuts, 240 E. Linwood, Kansas City, MO 64111, 931-5166. Famous food and travel writers across the country have touted the glories of Lamar's mouthwatering donut selection, and so will your kids. The famous foot-long glazed twists usually sell out fast, so get here early and bring a sweet tooth.

Murray's Ice Creams and Cookies, 4120 Pennsylvania, Kansas City, MO 64111, 931-5646. This true homemade ice cream usually pleases aficionados who want only the best. For kids there's a half-price double dip cone and delicious waffle cones dipped while warm in white chocolate and rolled in crushed candies. Yummy for the tummy.

Price Candy Company, 500 Nichols Rd., Seville Square, Kansas City, MO 64112, 561-8141. From annaclairs and pecan turks to chocolate-covered pretzels, kids have a ball choosing their favorites.

Panache, 4709 Central, Kansas City, MO 64111, 931-3191. Among the shop's gourmet treats for kids are chocolate stars, cars, teddy bears and edible chocolate birthday cards.

Russell Stover Candies, 320 Nichols Rd., Kansas City, MO 64111, (main office phone 842-9240). This locally-owned company has several locations around the city. Chocolates, bon bons, jelly beans and other sweets are children's choices.

T. J. Cinnamons, 800 W. 47th, Kansas City, MO 64112, 931-9341. (Several locations in Greater Kansas City. See Listing, Overland Park, KS.)

Topsy's, 214 Nichols Rd., Kansas City, MO 64112, 753-7373. Flavored popcorn, rich fudge and creamy ice cream are the hallmarks of this popular store with locations in most major shopping centers.

What's The Scoop?, 432 Westport Rd., Kansas City, MO 64111, 531-4060. This gourmet ice cream store includes a rotating list of 60 flavors that include everything from peanut butter truffle to triple chip.

SOUTH OF PLAZA (50TH ST. TO 125TH ST.)

ASSISTANCE

Special Assistance for the Disabled

The Whole Person, Inc., 6301 Rockhill Rd., Suite 305E, Kansas City, MO 64131, 361-0304 (VOICE); 361-7749 (TTY). This private not-for-profit organization helps people with disabilities. Its many services include *Access Kansas City,* a guide for disabled Kansas Citians that lists accommodations for those with mobility, visual and hearing impairments. Included in the book are accessible attractions and public buildings. The organization also has a newsletter of activities and disability-related information.

Direction Service Center. (See Listing under Special Assistance for the Disabled, Independence, MO.) This agency publishes a pamphlet featuring summer programs for disabled children.

HISTORIC SITES AND MUSEUMS

Alexander Major House, 8201 State Line Rd., Kansas City, MO 64114, 333-5556. Majors, whose freighting firms paved the way west, built his farmhouse in 1856 as the earliest headquarters for the Pony Express. The home is open for tours. There's lots of Pony Express paraphernalia inside for kids. *Time Frame:* 45 minutes. Ages: 2nd through 6th grade. *Important to Know:* (I) (G/R) ($) (B)

The Toy and Miniature Museum, 5235 Oak St., Kansas City, MO 64110, 333-2055. Young and old alike enjoy this fascinating collection of antique toys, exact-scale miniature doll houses and furnishings and large-scale working train. *Time Frame:* 45 minutes. *Ages:* pre-schoolers up. *Important to Know:* call to make sure it's open before you go. (I) (G/R) ($) (B)

UMKC Geosciences Museum, Geophysics Building, 1710 E. 52nd St., Kansas City, MO 64110, 276-1334. The museum displays a variety of unusual rocks and minerals, plus gemstones, fossils, petrified wood and sea shells. Of particular interest to kids is a set of rocks with water bubbles inside them. They can rotate the rods running through the rocks and watch the bubbles move. *Time Frame:* 30 minutes. *Ages:* K up. *Important to Know:* this would be a good tour to match up with a UMKC's observatory visit. (I) (G/R) (No $) (B)

THE ARTS

Camellot Academy, 11500 State Line Rd., Kansas City, MO 64114, 491-0333; 491-3090. Situated on the grounds of Barstow School, the performing arts camp is designed to bring out children's natural talents by offering classes in drama, arts and crafts, dance, and music, plus field trips and picnics. *Ages:* K through 8th grade. *Important to Know:* June/July programs are offered. (I/R) ($) (B)

Creative Dramatics, University of Missouri-Kansas City, Rm. 113, Royal Hall, Kansas City, MO 64110, 649-6912. The program is a collection of improvisational workshops that stress developmental drama. This is a good foundation for kids who want to take their talents further. *Ages:* 6 to 15. *Important to Know:* (I/R) ($) (B)

Dance Studio One, 600 W. 103rd St., Suite 103, Kansas City, MO 64114, 941-3990. Classes in ballet, tap, and jazz are taught by Liz Kelley, a former member of the Golddiggers of Dean Martin television show fame. Students perform in yearly recitals as well as benefit performances around the city. *Ages:* 3 up. *Important to Know:* (G/R) ($) (B)

Tiffany's Attic, 5028 Main and **The Waldo Astoria,** 7428 Washington, 561-7529. These professional theaters operated by the same management provide family plays and musicals that often appeal to children. Dinner is served prior to the show. *Time Frame:* 2 hours. *Ages:* 7 up. *Important to Know:* (I/R) (G/R)´($) (B)

University of Missouri-Kansas City Conservatory of Music, 4949 Cherry, Kansas City, MO 64110, 276-2730, 276-2700. The Conservatory holds concerts throughout the year featuring chamber music, jazz, classic and original dance choreography. Older children who are interested in music and dance can see talented aspiring professionals at work. Performances are given in an informal setting that provides a cozy, relaxed atmosphere for youngsters. *Time Frame;* 30 minutes to 1½ hours. *Ages:* 9 up. *Important to Know:* (I/R) (G/R) ($ and No $) (B)

AMUSEMENTS

Center Stage, 5600 E. Bannister Rd., (Bannister Mall), Kansas City, MO 64137, 761-7474. Kids can pretend they're rock stars and choose their favorite hits, singing along with the lead singer. On playback, they'll get a cassette with only their voices recorded, making their very own tape to give to family and friends. *Ages:* all. *Important to Know:* (I) ($) (No B)

Fun Factory, 5600 E. Bannister Rd. (Bannister Mall), Kansas City, MO 64137, 761-2611. The center has a carnival-like atmosphere complete with ski ball, kiddie rides, and video games. Winners get tickets which can be redeemed for prizes. *Ages:* all. *Important to Know:* No food, drink or chewing gum allowed. No concessions. (No B)

THE GREAT OUTDOORS

Kansas City, Missouri, Parks and Recreation
Department, 5605 E. 63rd St., Kansas City, MO 64130, 444-3113. (See Assistance, East of Plaza.)

Special Area Parks and Playgrounds

Most area parks offer picnic areas, ball fields, tennis courts, playgrounds, shelters and more. Some have drop-in program activities that include arts, crafts, and games. Most have bathrooms. Phone the Kansas City, MO, Parks and Recreation Department for information. (See Assistance, East of Plaza.) In the meantime, here's a sampling of what you'll find:

Arbor Villa Park, Main St. and 66th Terr.

Arno Park, 69th and Ward Parkway.

Bryant School, 57th and Wornall.

Holmes Park, 70th and Holmes.

Ingles School, 11600 Food Lane.

Loose Park, **52nd and Wornall Rd.** Has a wading pool, duck pond, a rose garden and garden center, and a fragrance garden for the sight-impaired.

Santa Fe School, 8908 Old Santa Fe Rd.

St. Regis School, 8941 James A. Reed Rd.

St. Thomas More, 118th St. and Holmes Rd.

Sunnyside Park, 82nd and Summit.

Sycamore Terr., 108th and Sycamore.

Tower Park, 75th and Holmes.

Summer Camping Programs

Barstow Summer Program, 11511 State Line Rd., Kansas City, MO 64114, 942-3255. Half-day sessions include sports clinics, academic courses, arts and crafts and more. *Ages:* K to 12. *Important to Know:* (I/R) ($) (B)

Operation Discovery, 8030 Ward Pkwy. Plaza, Kansas City, MO 64114, 333-5135. The day-long classes base their activities around a variety of themes. Games, arts and crafts, and music are part of the fun. *Ages:* 2 to 12. *Important to Know:* (I/R) ($) (B)

Pembroke Country Day School Summer Camp, 400 W. 51st St., Kansas City, MO 64112, 753-1300. The modestly priced day sessions occupy kids with painting, swimming, drama, archery, puppet-making, field trips, and more. *Ages:* K to 6th grade. *Important to Know:* (I/R) ($) (B)

ENTERTAINING PEOPLE

Emeline Dobbins Productions, 23 W. 69th St., Kansas City, MO 64113, 363-1358. Emeline Dobbins offers entertaining puppet shows for birthdays and special occasions and has a wide selection of classic plays, folktales and marionette variety shows tailored for your age group. *Ages:* all. *Important to Know:* (G/R) ($)

Midwest Storytelling Theater, 9100 Cherry, Kansas City, MO 64131, 444-5537. Sylvia Scott brings her Storytelling Concerts to your home for special occasions. She encourages children to be more creative and imaginative as they listen to her folk literature derived from many cultures. The experience is educational as well as fun. *Ages:* 4 up. *Important to Know:* (G/R) ($) (B)

SPECIAL ACTIVITIES

Dunn's Cider Mill, 171st and Holmes, Belton, MO 64012, 331-7214. Enjoy free samples of delicious natural cider and watch apples being pressed at the mill during apple season. Other treats include apple dumplings and cider donuts made fresh daily. Fun activities for kids: a Cider Sipoff in September and Scarecrow Contest around Halloween. The mill also provides a backroads map to scenic places in the area. *Ages:* all. *Important to Know:* (I) (G) ($ for food) (B)

SPECIAL EVENTS CALENDAR

JULY

Summer Daze, Loose Park, 51st and Wornall, sponsored by Kansas City, Missouri, Parks and Recreation, 274-1671. This annual event attracts thousands of kids ages 14 and under and feature a variety of games and fun. Special activities include a water slide, mud pit and moon walk. Pack a lunch for this day-long session. *Important to Know:* (No $)

EAST OF PLAZA (TROOST TO BLUE RIDGE BLVD.)

ASSISTANCE

Parks and Recreation Departments

Kansas City, Missouri, Parks and Recreation Department, 5605 E. 63rd St., Kansas City, MO 64130, 444-3113. (Also see The Great Outdoors.) Because of space limitations, it's impossible for us to list the wealth of parks, playgrounds, community centers, sports activities, day camps, summer drop-in programs and cultural offerings. For more information about what's available in your area phone the number listed: Community Centers, Swimming and Boating, 274-1671; Special Recreation, Cultural Activities, Sunday Night Concert Series, Games and Sports, 444-3113; Outdoor Education, 444-4363.

Special Assistance for the Disabled, Kansas City, Missouri, Parks and Recreation Department, 5605 E. 63rd St., Kansas City, MO 64130, 444-3113. The department features recreation programs for the physically and mentally disabled that includes Special Olympics, sports leagues, summer dances, picnics and outings. They also have a slide show on recreational opportunities for the disabled.

Clubs and Organizations

Boys and Girls Clubs of Greater Kansas City. (See Assistance, Downtown Kansas City, MO.)

Heart of America Council, Boy Scouts of America. (See Assistance, Kansas City, KS.)

Kansas City, Missouri, Council of Camp Fire, 8733 Sni-A-Bar Rd., Kansas City, MO 64129, 737-3256. Co-educational group activity programs for school-aged children stress self-reliance and decision-making skills in a fun, informal atmosphere. Resident and weekend camping programs teach youngsters how to enjoy the beauty of nature and preserve it for the future. Camp Fire self-reliance courses educate kids about the basics of safety, good citizenship skills, responsibility and assertiveness. *Ages:* K-12th Grade. *Important to Know:* (I) ($) (D)

Mid-Continent Council of Girl Scouts, 8383 Blue Parkway Dr., Kansas City, MO 64133, 348-8750. An extension of the largest girl's organization in the world, the Mid-Continent Council provides opportunities and activities that develop skills in decision-making, leadership, career development, environmental awareness and recreation. Developing self-potential and high ethical values are stressed. Activities are centered around out-of-doors camping and sports, health and well-being, learning about people, career exploration, and the arts. The groups are headed by an adult leader who acts as a role model. *Ages:* K-12th grade. *Important to Know:* (I) ($) (D)

YMCA of Greater Kansas City. (See Clubs and Organizations, Midtown Kansas City, MO.)

BUSINESS AND COMMERCIAL TOURS

Starlight Theatre, Swope Park, Kansas City, MO 64132, 333-9481. Spring and summer tours are offered and include a visit to the dressing rooms, wardrobe, orchestra pit, stage and backstage areas. You could plan a trip in conjunction with a family-oriented production the day before or after the performance. *Time Frame:* 30 minutes. *Ages:* 6 to teens. *Important to Know;* (G/R) (No $) (B)

HISTORIC SITES AND MUSEUMS

Black Archives of Mid-America, 2033 Vine, Kansas City, MO 64109, 483-1300. The archives hold one of the country's most complete collections of paintings and sculptures by black artists. There is information about black musicians, writers, and local black leaders. Exhibits trace the history of blacks in Kansas City. *Time Frame:* 40 minutes. *Ages:* 2nd grade up. *Important to Know:* (I) (G/R) ($) (B)

Cave Spring Interpretive Center, 8701 E. Gregory, (Corner of Gregory Blvd. and Blue Ridge Cut-Off), Kansas City, MO 64133, 358-2283. This historic campground on the Oregon-Santa Fe Trail has a small cave and spring that supplied pioneers with their cooking water. It features a nature center, hiking trails, crafts classes, science lectures and field trips. Call for a copy of their schedule. *Time Frame:* one hour; the walking trail can be covered in 15 minutes. *Ages:* 1st grade up. *Important to Know:* (I) (G/R) (No $) (B) (D)

THE ARTS

Starlight Theatre, 4600 Starlight Rd., Kansas City, MO 64132, 333-9481. Families can sit under the stars in warm weather and enjoy a variety of concerts and Broadway musicals. *Time Frame:* about 2 hours. *Ages:* 7 up. *Important to Know:* (I/R) (G/R) ($—50% discount in Mezzanine and Terrace levels for any Broadway Musical show with Y.A. Arts Card which is good through all Starlight Theater ticket outlets) (B) (D)

AMUSEMENTS

Benjamin's Stables, 6401 E. 87th St., Kansas City, MO 64138, 761-5055. Here's a taste of the country for kids of all ages. In summer hayrides are available; winter brings sleigh rides. There's a party barn, shelter house for picnics, and parties and an annual rodeo. Not to mention horseback riding by the hour, with private and group classes available. *Ages:* 3 up. Important to Know: (I/R) (G/R) ($) (B) (D)

Swope Park Boathouse, Swope Park Lagoon, Kansas City132, 274-1671. There are paddle boats and canoes to rent by the hour, plus rides on the excursion boat, "The Clipper," which runs Memorial Day to Labor Day weekends. There's plenty of fun for kids at very reasonable prices. *Time Frame:* 1 hour. *Ages:* all. *Important to Know:* (I) (G/R) (B) (D)

Kansas City Zoo, Swope Park, Meyer Blvd. and Swope Pkwy., Kansas City, MO 64132, 333-7406. Sprawling across

80 acres in the heart of Swope Park, the zoo contains hundreds of domestic and exotic animals. Children's favorites include the petting zoo, a dairy barn with milking demonstrations, a miniature train ride, baby animal nursery, elephant, camel and pony rides and educational training sessions with elephants and sea lions. The zoo also offers catered group picnics for children and adults. The kiddie menu is the usual hot dogs and sodas, with upscale picnic fixings for parents upon request. *Ages:* all. *Important to Know:* (I) (G) ($) (B) (D)

SPORTS

Boxing Center, 3700 Woodland, Kansas City, MO 64109, 924-9957, 444-3113. Parks and Recreation's award-winning boxing program is available for boys who want to perfect their skills and participate in silver mittens. Each boy gets to experience a match. *Ages:* 6 to 16. *Important to Know:* (I/R) (No $) (B)

Kansas City Royals, Royals Stadium, I-70 and Blue Ridge Cutoff, P.O. Box 419969, Kansas City, MO 64141, 921-4400. The stadium is home to the American League's Kansas City Royals, always favorites with the kids. Infants and toddlers under 32 inches tall get in free. *Important to Know:* (I/R) (G/R) ($) (B)

Kansas City Chiefs, Arrowhead Stadium, I-70 and Blue Ridge Cutoff, 1 Arrowhead Drive, Kansas City, MO 64129, 924-9300. The team plays two pre-season and eight regular-season games each year. There are special ticket prices for students 17 and under. *Important to Know:* (I/R) (G/R) ($) (B)

Swope Park Pool, Lewis Rd. and Riverside, mailing address Kansas City, Missouri, Parks and Recreation, 1722 E. 17th Terr., Kansas City, MO 64108, 274-1671. Swimming lessons for toddlers to advanced swimmers are held here in 2-week sessions. Classes in rhythmic water exercise, lifesaving, diving and Red Cross certified safety instruction are also offered. Parents must accompany aqua tots into the pool. *Ages:* toddlers to adults. *Important to Know:* (I/R) ($)(B)

PLAYING TOGETHER

Camp Lake of the Woods Riding Academy, 5600 E. Gregory Blvd., Kansas City, MO 64132, 444-4375. (Also see The Great Outdoors, Special Programs and Exhibits, East of Plaza.) Horseback riding lessons are offered for children. Parents may also take lessons along with their kids. There are pony rides for pre-schoolers. *Ages:* 7 to adult. *Important to Know:* (I/R) ($) (B) (D)

Cave Spring Interpretive Center, 8701 E. Gregory, (Corner of Gregory Blvd. and Blue Ridge Cut-Off), Kansas City, MO 64133, 358-2283. (See Historic Sites and Museums, East of Plaza.) The center's special activities for kids and parents include family walks in the woods, night hikes, campfire storytelling, and programs on Indian lore.

Lakeside Nature Center, 5600 E. Gregory Blvd., Kansas City, MO 64132, 444-4656. (See Outdoor Education Programs, this section.)

Swope Park Pool, Lewis Rd. and Riverside, mailing address Kansas City, Missouri, Parks and Recreation, 1722 E. 17th Terr., Kansas City, MO 64108, 274-1671. (See Sports, this section.)

THE GREAT OUTDOORS

Kansas City, Missouri, Parks and Recreation
Department, 5605 E. 63rd St., Kansas City, MO 64130, 444-3113. (See Listing under Assistance, East'of Plaza.)

Special Programs and Exhibits

Camp Lake of the Woods Riding Academy, 5600 E. Gregory Blvd., Kansas City, MO 64132, 444-4375. (Also see Playing Together, East of Plaza.) Sponsored by the Kansas City, MO, Parks and Recreation, this camp features western-style horseback riding lessons for youngsters, plus training clinics for grooming and showing horses. There are pony rides for pre-schoolers. *Ages:* 7 to adult. *Important to Know:* (I/R) ($) (B) (D)

Cave Spring Interpretive Center, 8701 E. Gregory, (Corner of Gregory Blvd. and Blue Ridge Cut-Off), Kansas City, MO 64133, 358-2283. (See Playing Together, East of Plaza.)

Gamestreet, Swope Park Entrance, Kansas City, Missouri, Parks and Recreation Department, 5605 E. 63rd St., Kansas City, MO 64130, 444-3113. This 200 ft. by 200 ft. multipurpose pad contains play areas for volleyball, horseshoes, roller skating, wheelchairs and organized games and is open May through September. *Important to Know:* (I/R) (G/R) (No $) (B) (D)

Missouri Department of Conservation, 8618 E. 63rd St., Kansas City, MO 64133, 356-2280. This agency has information on Conservation Department wildlife and nature areas. It also puts on several interpretive nature programs such as "Eagle Days," and "Prairie Days," designed to help children understand the environment around them. Live animals such as eagles are often used in the presentations. *Ages:* K up. *Important to Know:* (I/R) (G/R) (No $) (No B)

Safety Village, Swope Park Entrance, Kansas City, Missouri, Parks and Recreation Department, 5605 E. 63rd St., Kansas City, MO 64130, 444-3113. This is a miniature town set up inside Gamestreet (see Special Programs and Exhibits, this section). It's designed to teach pre-schoolers the principles of safety for pedestrians and drivers. Officer Friendly of the Kansas City, Missouri, Police Department teaches traffic safety to tykes on 3-wheelers, guiding them through the village which is open May through September. *Ages:* 3 to 5. *Important to Know;* (I/R) (G/R) (No $) (B) (D)

Special Area Parks and Playgrounds

Most area parks offer picnic areas, ball fields, tennis courts, playgrounds, shelters and more. There are some playgrounds with drop-in program activities that include arts, crafts, and games. Most have bathrooms. Phone the Kansas City, MO, Parks and Recreation Department for information. (See Assistance, East of Plaza.) In the meantime, here's a sampling of what you'll find:

Blenheim School, 2411 E. 70th Terr.

Blue Hills Park, 53rd and Brooklyn.

Faxon School, 3701 Paseo.

Greenwood School, 27th and Cleveland.

Milton Moore School, 4510 Linwood.

Richardson School, 36th and Park.

Swope Park, 5600 E. Gregory Blvd. The second largest city park in the nation, Swope Park includes a lagoon with excursion and rental boats, a nature center with guided nature trail hikes and classes, the Kansas City Zoo, Starlight Theatre, golf courses, a swimming pool, a riding academy, camps, greenhouses, a pavilion, a Folf (Frisbee golf) course, and Gamestreet, a multi-purpose recreational pad and more.

Pinkerton School, 6409 Agnes.

Troost School, 60th and Forest.

Outdoor Education Programs

Kansas City Zoo Wild, Kansas City Zoo, Swope Park, Meyer Blvd. and Swope Pkwy., Kansas City, MO 64132, 333-7406. (Also see Zoo School, Outdoor Education Programs.) This 3-day educational program features animals, animal games and animal snacks and is an excellent way to introduce kids to the zoo. Tailored to the needs of younger children, "Zoo Wild" is different from the "Zoo School." (See Zoo School this section.) *Ages:* 5 to 8. *Important to Know:* (I) (G) ($) (B)

Lakeside Nature Center, 5600 E. Gregory Blvd., Kansas City, MO 64132, 444-4656. The center has year-around classes for children and parents. There are tours of the center, plus bird walks, wildflower classes, fossil walks, and nature hikes. Parents and older children can also be part of the nature center's volunteer activities, which include the care and feeding or orphaned birds. *Ages:* pre-school up. *Important to Know:* (I/R) (G/R) ($ for mini classes) (B) (D)

Outdoor School, 5605 E. 63rd St., Kansas City, MO 64130, 444-4363. The school has a 4-hour workshop deep in the Swope Park woods that teaches natural history lessons. This in-depth experience is more than a nature walk and takes the kids back into terrain that is inaccessible except on foot. There are different versions for different age groups. *Ages:* pre-school up. *Important to Know:* parents can volunteer to accompany the group into the woods. (G/R) ($) (B)

Zoo School, Kansas City Zoo, Swope Park, Meyer Blvd. and Swope Pkwy, Kansas City, MO 64132, 333-7405. (Also see Kansas City Zoo Wild under Outdoor Education Programs, this section.) Offered by the Zoo's education department and run by volunteer docents, the educational day camp holds June classes featuring the Zoo Discovery Lab. Here children study the plant and animal kingdoms including fossils and animal skeletons. The chance to learn about animals from zoo professionals is a rare opportunity for kids. *Time Frame:* day-long classes. *Ages:* 5 to 12. *Important to Know:* (I/R) ($) (B) (D)

Summer Camping Programs

Camp Rainbow Day Camp, Cave Spring Interpretive Center, 8701 E. Gregory Blvd., Kansas City, MO 64133, 358-2283. Camp Rainbow offers a creative atmosphere of fun and fresh air for the physically and mentally disabled. The supervised 4-day programs include arts and crafts, games, songs, and nature study. Kids bring a sack lunch. Sessions separate the mentally and physically disabled. *Ages:* 6 up. *Important to Know:* ($) (D)

Rocky Point Day Camp, 5600 E. Gregory, Swope Park, **Kansas City, MO 64132, 444-4363.** This Kansas City, MO, Parks and Recreation day camp is American Camping Association certified. It features nature hikes and walks, swimming lessons, archery, arts and crafts and more in 2-week summer sessions. *Ages:* 7 to 12. *Important to Know:* (I) ($) (B)

SPECIAL ACTIVITIES

Camp Fire, 8733 Sni-A-Bar Rd., Kansas City, MO 64129, **737-3256.** The organization provides a series of courses for children that teaches both personal safety and responsible citizenship through games, read-aloud action stories, cartoon characters, and creative workshops. Invaluable for teaching kids to handle emergencies, the sessions offer parental follow-up and involvement. *Time Frame:* 45 minutes. *Ages:* 5 to 12. *Important to Know:* (I/R) (G/R) (No $)

Kansas City, Missouri, Parks and Recreation Community Centers, 274-1671. *The following community centers in this area provide after-school and Saturday classes and activities in a variety of sports and gym games, crafts and music classes for kids 3 up:*

Marlborough Community Center, 8204 Paseo, Kansas City, MO 64131, 444-2078.

Southeast Community Center, 3601 E. 63rd St., Kansas City, MO 64130, 444-9080.

SPECIAL EVENTS CALENDAR

JUNE

Tom Watson Golf Clinic, PGA and Kansas City, Missouri, Parks and Recreation Department, 5605 E. 63rd St., Kansas City, MO 64130, 444-3113. Held in Swope Park each year, this is an all-day PGA Junior Golf Clinic for kids 7 to 18. Watson will be on hand to help the kids with tips and demonstrations. *Important to Know:* (No $)

JULY

Annual K.C. Rodeo, Benjamin Ranch, 6401 E. 87th St., Kansas City, MO 64138, 761-5055. The ranch hosts this rodeo each July 4th which is sponsored by the Professional Rodeo Cowboy Association as a benefit for the K.C. Jaycees. Professional riders and exciting stunts provide thrills for the whole family. *Important to Know:* ($) (D)

Fourth of July at Swope Park, Main Entrance, Kansas City, Missouri, Parks and Recreation Department, 5605 E. 63rd St., Kansas City, MO 64130, 444-3113. Children ages 6 to 11 can participate in games and contests throughout the day and watch the evening fireworks display. *Important to Know:* (No $)

AUGUST

Ethnic Enrichment Festival, Swope Park Pavilion, Kansas City, Missouri, Parks and Recreation Department,

5605 E. 63rd St., Kansas City, MO 64130, 444-3113. Designed to celebrate the rich heritage of Kansas City, the 3-day event features music, dance, crafts, and food from Kansas City's diverse ethnic communities. Children like the good eats and have fun learning how to trace their family tree. *Important to Know:* (No $)

JOHNSON COUNTY, KANSAS

OVERLAND PARK, LEAWOOD, FAIRWAY, PRAIRIE VILLAGE, SHAWNEE, MERRIAM, LENEXA, OLATHE, BUCYRUS, LOUISBURG, GARDNER, AND EDGERTON

KEY: (I) individual tours, no reservations needed; (I/R) individual tours, reservations needed; (G) group tours, no reservations needed; (G/R) group tours, reservations needed; ($) fee; (No $) no fee; (B) bathrooms; (No B) no bathrooms; (D) some accommodations for the disabled.

> *Johnson County comprises an immense expanse of suburban cities and townships that abound with plenty of interesting opportunities for children. The following is just a sampling of what's available here. For your convenience, we've grouped the cities together by their close proximity to one another. NOTE: Unless otherwise noted all Johnson County area codes are 913.*

OVERLAND PARK AND LEAWOOD

ASSISTANCE

Convention Bureaus and Chambers of Commerce

Overland Park Chamber of Commerce, 10975 Benson, Suite 350, Overland Park, KS 66210, 491-3600.

Overland Park Convention and Visitors Bureau,
10975 Benson, Suite 360, Overland Park, KS 66210, 491-0123.

Parks and Recreation Departments

Johnson County Parks and Recreation, 6501 Antioch,
Shawnee Mission, KS 66202, 831-3355.

Clubs and Organizations

Heart of America Council, Boy Scouts of America.
(See Assistance, Kansas City, KS.)

Sunflower Council of Camp Fire, Inc. (See Assistance,
Shawnee, KS.)

The Santa Fe Trail Council of Girl Scouts, Inc. (See
Assistance, Kansas City, KS.)

Mid-Continent Council of Girl Scouts. (See Assistance,
East of Plaza, Kansas City, MO.)

YMCA Of Greater Kansas City. (See Clubs and Organizations, Midtown, Kansas City, MO.)

BUSINESS AND COMMERCIAL TOURS

Inter-Collegiate Press, 6015 Travis Lane, **Shawnee
Mission, KS 66201, 432-8100.** A tour of the plant takes kids
from the production stages of a book to the end of the line
when publications are ready to be shipped. Everything from
paste-up to printing and binding is covered first-hand and
close-up. *Time Frame:* 45 min. *Ages:* junior to senior high
school students. *Important to Know:* (G/R) (No $) (B) (D)

THE ARTS

Young Audiences Arts Card, Kansas City Chapter of
Young Audiences™, (See The Arts, Midtown, Kansas City,
MO.)

American Dance Center, 11728 Quivira, Overland Park, **KS 66210, 451-3020.** Run by the directors of the American Youth Ballet, this not-for-profit dance company teaches tap, jazz, modern dance with an emphasis on ballet. *Ages:* preschool to high school. *Important to Know:* (I/R) ($) (B)

American Youth Ballet, 11728 Quivira, Overland Park, **KS 66210, 451-3020.** Comprised of young dancers aged 11 to 18, the ballet company is open by audition to students from around Kansas City. The students perform in major productions such as "Cinderella," and "Through the Looking Glass," given at the Folly Theater at Christmas time. *Important to Know:* There is a modest fee to attend the performances, which are suitable for children of all ages.

"Art Discovery" Summer Enrichment Program, Shawnee Mission South High School, 5800 W. 107th St., Overland Park, KS 66207, 648-3005. This summer program offers students art experiences designed to supplement and build upon those received during the regular school year. Hands-on activities include everything from print-making and drawing to computer graphics and sculpture. *Time Frame:* half or full days; week-long summer sessions. *Ages:* 1st through 6th grade. *Important to Know:* enroll early; space is limited. (I/R) ($) (B)

Janet Sanders Creative Dramatics, (Address varies), **531-3120.** Mrs. Sanders teaches art, literature and drama at area churches and schools. The courses allow children to use their creativity and have fun with literature. The unusual classes also afford kids the opportunity to perform before friends and peers. Mrs. Sanders tells the kids a story which they then act out. Costumes, props and crafts are utilized in the performances. *Time Frame:* 2-hour sessions, one day a week. *Ages:* 3 to 13. *Important to Know:* (I/R) (G/R) ($)

Jack and Jill Players, 3621 W. 95th St., Overland Park, **KS 66206, 649-0308.** The school features basic training in the performing arts, including jazz and tap dancing, improvisation, drama and voice, and strives to build a student's self-confidence and poise. The company produces variety shows and children's fantasies. *Ages;* 7 through high school. **Important to Know:** (I/R) ($) (B)

Johnson County Community College Youth Pro-grams, **12345 College Blvd. at Quivira Rd., Overland Park, KS 66210, 469-2323.** The program strives to stimulate creativity and expand growth opportunities in the arts and academic areas. Courses include everything from "Clay for Kids," to "Let's Pretend." There are also accelerated classes for high-ability students. *Ages:* 1st to 9th grade. *Important to Know:* (I/R) ($) (B) (D)

"Miss Jackie" Weissman, 10001 El Monte, Overland Park, KS 66207, 381-3672. A nationally recognized education expert, musician, composer, lecturer and personality, Miss Jackie's school concerts are well known locally and children actively participate in her educational "Sing Around The World" and "Mornings with Music" concerts for pre-school and kindergarten kids. Miss Jackie also features family and parent programs and offers a catalog of Early Childhood Music Materials and Programs that showcase song, activity and picture books, recordings, plus audio and video cassettes for parents, teachers and children. *Ages:* tots up. *Important to Know:* (G/R) ($)

"Music Enrichment," Summer Enrichment Program, Shawnee Mission South High School, 5800 W. 107th St., Overland Park, KS 66207, 648-3005; 831-1900. Children are introduced to a variety of music through participation in games and musical performances. Activities involve students with musical instruments, computers, games and singing. *Ages:* 1st to 6th grade. *Important to Know:* enroll early; space is limited. (I/R) ($) (B)

Music in Miniature (The Gant Sisters), 95th and Mission, Ranch Mart North, P.O. Box 6437, Leawood, KS 66206, 383-1533. The Gant Sisters' cultural enrichment program centers around music and drama for children. The school provides a fantasy-like atmosphere replete with color, puppets, rainbows and balloons. The kids perform on a miniature stage, reading music and learning about Bach and Beethoven. Pioneers in the field of children's music, the Gant Sisters offer albums and song books featuring their work. *Ages:* 3 to 6. Important to Know: (I/R) ($) (B)

Overland Park Arts Commission, 6300 W. 87th St., Overland Park, KS 66212, 381-5252. Among its varied cultural programs, the commission sponsors the Overland Park Children's Choir and family-oriented free outdoor summer concerts. Call for details.

Sunshine Generation, 10510 W. 90th St., Overland Park, KS 66214, 894-6934. Classes in basic performance skills such as voice, music theory, dance and showmanship are offered at six locations. *Ages:* 3 to 15. *Important to Know:* (I/R) ($) (B)

Theatre for Young America, 7204 W. 80th St., Overland Park, KS 62604, 648-4600. The only equity children's theater in the Midwest adapts favorite children's stories for the stage and gives performances during the school year. *Time Frame:* 1 hour. *Ages:* pre-school through 8th grade. *Important to Know:* (I/R) (G/R) (half off weekend performances with Y.A. Arts Card) (B) (D)

Theater for Young America Acting School, 7204 West 80th St., Overland Park, KS 66204, 648-4600. The school features a variety of theater classes that help develop poise, confidence, creativity and skill. Courses are geared to the age and level of experience and include everything from creative dramatics to actual play production. The workshops help develop skills at putting on public performances for community events. *Ages:* 3 to adult. *Important to Know:* (I/R) ($) (B) (D)

AMUSEMENTS

Malibu Grand Prix, 11200 W. 87th St., Overland Park, KS 66214, 492-4949. A race track for go-carts and formula cars gives older kids an opportunity to drive the cars around the track in a relatively safe, controlled environment. Children must be at least 4'6" to drive and wear a helmet and seat belt. There are birthday packages including rides, tokens for games, and private party space. *Ages:* 8 up. *Important to Know:* (I) (G/R) ($) (B)

Putt-Putt Golf and Games, 6845 W. 91st St., Overland Park, KS 66212, 642-8282. This outdoor miniature golf facility holds three courses of varying degrees of difficulty. There's also an indoor game room and party packages are available. *Ages:* all. *Important to Know:* (I) (G/R) ($) (B)

SPORTS

Heartland School of Riding, 13333 Antioch Rd., Overland Park, KS 66213, 897-3939. Heartland's professional instructors work with the special needs of emotionally, mentally and physically disabled children, teaching them how to ride. Sessions run from March through December. *Time Frame:* 1 hour a week. *Ages:* 6 up. *Important to Know:* (I/R) (G/R) ($) (B) (D)

Hershey Track and Field, held at Johnson County Community College, Quivira and College Blvd. (Mailing address, Johnson County Parks and Recreation, 6501 Antioch, Shawnee Mission, KS 66202, 831-3355). The June meet encourages children to participate in track and field activities. Kansas youngsters can enter either two track and one field, or two field and one track event. Ribbons are awarded to winners. *Ages:* 6 to 14. *Important to Know:* (I) (No $) (B)

Indian Creek Bike/Hike Trail, extends from Indian Valley Park at 116th St. and U.S. Alt. 69 to Foxhill South Park at 109th and Mission. Young children can accompany parents along this trail that connects 13 different park areas in an 8-mile area. Teens and adults with driver's license I.D. may rent bicycles for trail use at Indian Creek Recreation Center, 103rd and Marty. *Ages:* all. *Important to Know:* this trail connects with Leawood's Tomahawk Creek Greenway. (I) (G) ($ for bicycle rental) (No B)

Indian Valley Stables, 3504 College Blvd., Overland Park, KS 66211, 491-9924. The stable boards horses and gives riding lessons for children. *Time Frame:* 1 hour lesson. *Ages:* 8 up. *Important to Know:* (I/R) (G/R) ($) (B)

Sports Clinics For Youth, Johnson County Community College, 12345 College Blvd. at Quivira Rd., Overland Park, KS 66210, 469-3823. A variety of week-long sports clinics are held here as part of the Continuing Education, Community Services Program for youngsters. The intensive-training experience also affords kids an opportunity to make new friends in a college campus setting. *Time Frame:* 4 to 6 hours daily. *Ages:* 7 to 18. *Important to Know:* (I/R) ($) (B)

St. Andrews Golf Course, 11099 W. 135th St., Overland Park, KS 66221, 897-3804. Junior golfers can putt around on this scenic course. Golf lessons are available for youngsters who may participate in a free tournament held at the Overland Park Golf Club each August. Patron cards are available for residents and non-residents of Overland Park. *Ages:* 6 to 17. *Important to Know:* (I/R) ($) (B)

Overland Park Golf Club, 12600 Quivira Rd., Overland Park, KS 66213, 897-3809. Children are welcome to play on the full 18-hole course as well as a 9-hole par 3 course. Junior golf lessons are available for ages 6 to 17. A free tournament is held here each August for kids ages 4 to 17. *Important to Know:* (I/R) ($) (B)

Swimming, Overland Park Pools, City of Overland Park Leisure Services, 6300 W. 87th St., Overland Park, KS 66212, 381-5252. Six fully-staffed public pools offer summertime fun for kids. The Overland Park Municipal Swim and Diving Teams provide youngsters an opportunity to compete with youths from other area city teams. Lessons are available. *Ages:* all. *Important to Know:* (I) (G) ($) (B)

Tennis, City of Overland Park Leisure Services, 6300 W. 87th St., Overland Park, KS 66212, 381-5252. There are 29 courts located throughout the city. Group and private lessons are offered for beginners and experienced players. *Ages:* 8 to 16. *Important to Know:* (I/R) (G/R) ($) (B)

Tomahawk Creek Greenway, from Leawood Park to 123rd and Mission, City of Leawood, 9617 Lee Blvd., Leawood, KS 66206, 642-5555. This pathway leaves the west end of Leawood Park and heads south, crossing Indian and Toma- hawk Creeks. You and the kids can bike, hike, jog or horse- back ride along this scenic route that winds through the area. A nature trail booklet and map is available from the City of Leawood. *Ages:* all. *Important to Know:* (I) (G) (No $) (No B)

THE GREAT OUTDOORS

Special Programs and Exhibits

Johnson County Parks and Recreation, 6501 Antioch Rd., Shawnee Mission, KS 66202, 831-3355. Courses in gymnastics for babies and toddlers are just part of the extensive offerings. Quarterly brochures give detailed listings for children's activities. *Ages:* all. *Important to Know:* (I/R) (G/R) ($) (B)

Special Area Parks and Playgrounds

There are many parks located in the cities of Overland Park and Leawood. Most are equipped with picnic areas, ball fields, tennis courts, playgrounds, shelters, bathrooms and more. Phone or write the Johnson County Parks and

Recreation (see Assistance, Overland Park, KS) for a complete listing of parks in your area. In the meantime here are a few of the larger ones:

Indian Creek Recreation Center, 103rd and Marty, Overland Park, KS.

The center is located along the Overland Park Bike/Hike Trail. Tennis courts are a big attraction here and there are lessons for all ages.

Leawood City Park, 10600 Lee Boulevard, Leawood, KS.

There's an Olympic-size diving pool, intermediate and wading pools, plus fitness and tennis courts, multifaceted playground, and access to the Tomahawk Creek Greenway. Memberships for pool and court use.

Overland Park Community Park, 135th and Switzer, Overland Park, KS.

Adjacent to the Deanna Rose Farmstead, the park also features unique play structures for young children.

Roe Park, 104th and Roe, Overland Park, KS.

The park has a large pool and wading pool. A circular bike/jogging trail gives youngsters an opportunity to exercise on the path without ever leaving their parent's sight.

South Lake Park, 86th and Valleyview, Overland Park, KS.

With two fishing docks and a well-stocked lake, the park is an ideal place for a family outing. There's a circular path for biking, jogging or walking and elaborate play structures for the toddlers.

Nature Sanctuaries

Deanna Rose Memorial Farmstead, 138th and Switzer, in the Overland Park Community Park, Overland Park, KS 66221, 381-5252, Ext. 740.

(Also see Summer Camping Programs this section.) The miniature farmstead includes a petting farm for children complete with garden plots, silo and barn. Domestic animals such as ducks, horses, goats, chickens, pigs and rabbits are housed here as well as eagles, owls, peacocks and buffalo. Adjacent to the Farmstead are self-guided nature trails for walking. *Ages:* all. *Important to Know:* (I) (G/R) (No $) (B) (D)

Outdoor Education Programs

Outdoor Recreation and Education for Young Groups, Johnson County Parks and Recreation, 6501 Antioch, Shawnee Mission, KS 66202, 888-3355. Park rangers and naturalists teach seasonal group nature classes here. There's canoeing in the spring, hayriding in fall, and snowshoe hiking in winter for kids and parents. *Ages:* 6 to teens. *Important to Know:* (G/R) ($) (B)

Outdoor Education Laboratory, Shawnee Mission South High School, 5800 W. 107th St., Overland Park, KS 66207, 236-7344. Children from all school districts may enroll in this exciting program that provides kids with nature and science activities combined with recreational swimming and games. *Time Frame:* full day week-long sessions in summer. *Ages:* 1st through 6th grades. Important to Know: bus transportation to the laboratory's nature centers is provided from two locations. (I/R) ($) (B)

Shawnee Mission Enrichment Programs—Nature and Science, Art, History, Drama and Physical Education—Shawnee Mission South High School, 5800 W. 107th St., Overland Park, KS 66207, 648-3005. Open to kids from all school districts, the summer program offers sessions in hands-on nature and science experiences such as bird walks and reptile study. Art courses focus on everything from architecture to working with clay. Classes in history showcase activities centered around such topics as native

North Americans and archeological digs. The drama curriculum involves theatrical productions, make-up, acting and set design. Physical Education topics promote fitness, fun and good health with activities such as fencing, archery, kickball, and aerobics. *Time Frame:* half or full day week-long sessions. *Ages:* 1st through 6th grades. *Important to Know:* early registration is essential. (I/R) ($) (B) (D)

Summer Camping Programs

Camp Loads of Fun, New Horizons Summer Program, Johnson County Parks and Recreation, 6501 Antioch, Shawnee Mission, KS 66202, 831-3355. The summer camp is held at several Johnson County locations and features day-long activities, crafts, games, sports, swimming, field trips and more. Early and late drop-off and pick-up is available for working parents. *Ages:* 6 to 18. *Important to Know:* (I/R) ($) (B) (D)

Farmstead Day Camp, Deanna Rose Farmstead, 137th and Switzer, Overland Park, KS 66221, 381-5252. Two week-long summer sessions are offered at this miniature farmstead. Activities include games, arts, crafts and outdoor fun. *Ages:* 5 to 8. *Important to Know:* (I/R) ($) (B) (D)

Outdoor Discovery Camp, Johnson County Parks and Recreation, 6501 Antioch, Shawnee Mission, KS 66202, 831-3355. Held at Shawnee Mission Park in Shawnee or Heritage Park in Olathe, the program features park naturalists and rangers who offer courses centering around such themes as survival skills, wildlife discovery, water, and more. There are plenty of hands-on experiences with hiking, crafts, and animals. *Ages:* 8 to 12. *Important to Know:* (I/R) ($) (B)

SPECIAL LIBRARY PROGRAMS

Parent/Child Learning Centers, Johnson County Libraries (Oak Park, Lackman, Corinth, Antioch, Cedar Roe) P.O. Box 2901, Shawnee Mission, KS 66201, 831-1550. Designed for parent/child participation in early reading experiences, the libraries offer theme-based stations that include hands-on training utilizing everything from educational toys, music and games, to sensory awareness and picture concepts. *Time Frame:* 1 hour or more. *Ages:* the program is designed for pre-schoolers, but infants and toddlers are welcome. *Important to Know:* (I) (No $) (B) (D— except for Corinth)

ENTERTAINING PEOPLE

Animal Fantasies, phone only, 541-1121. The company provides big, furry party animals for youngsters. Kids interact with the cuddly critters, playing games and participating in music and craft activities. *Ages:* 2 to 6. *Important to Know:* (G/R) ($)

Dreams Come True—Creative Parties for Children, phone only, 341-6991. For special occasions this "Theme Party" entertainment features delightful inside-the-home parties for kids such as a Teddy Bear Tea, Fairy Princess Fantasy, and Hunny Bunny's Posh Pageant. Kids participate in the fun by dressing up in costume, singing, dancing, and playing games. *Ages:* 2 to 12. *Important to Know:* (G/R) ($)

SPECIAL ACTIVITIES

Overland Park Community Center, 6300 W. 87th St., Overland Park, KS 66212, 381-5252. Programs include workshops for kids, an Easter egg hunt, Halloween parties, sports classes and more. *Ages:* all. *Important to Know:* (I/R) (G/R) ($) (B)

Pretty As A Picture, 11440 W. 104th St., Overland Park, KS 66214, 541-9099. If your daughter's social graces resemble that of a punk rocker, perhaps you might consider this interesting alternative. Young ladies are taught the basics of etiquette in a genteel setting, where nary a rude or ill-tempered word is heard. Girls learn about poise and personal grooming and receive a certificate upon completion of the 7-week course. *Time Frame:* hour class session. *Ages:* 6 to 16. *Important to Know:* (I/R) ($) (B)

U.S. Toy, Co., 2008 W. 103rd Terr., Leawood, KS 66206, 642-8247. This warehouse of toys and novelties also features art supplies, costumes, magic shop items, play equipment, books, party items and carnival prizes. It's also an outlet for Creative Playthings toys and games. *Time Frame:* 1 hour. *Ages:* infants to adults. *Important to Know:* Keep a watch on the kids since it's easy to get lost here. Unsupervised children under age 5 aren't allowed in certain areas. (I) (G) ($) (B)

SPECIAL EVENTS

JUNE-JULY

Overland Park Band Concerts, Overland Park Arts Commission, 6300 W. 87th St., Overland Park, KS 66212, 381-5252. These open-air Sunday band concerts are great for family outings and feature some musical numbers especially for kids. (No $) (D)

OCTOBER

Safe Halloween Programs, Metcalf South Shopping Center, 9635 Metcalf, Overland Park, KS 66212, 649-2277; Oak Park Mall, 11461 W. 95th St., Overland Park, KS 66214, 888-4400. These malls offer alternatives to the somewhat risky neighborhood trick-or-treating. Merchants give goodies to costumed kids and special entertainment and refreshments are provided. (No $) (D)

FUN EATS

Fast Food Havens, 63rd Street from Mission Rd. to Antioch Rd. Everything from tacos, hamburgers and fried chicken to pizza and ice cream can be found along this busy street.

Fast Food Havens, Metcalf from 75th St. to 107th St. The Metcalf Strip features everything from barbecue and hamburger joints, to Mexican, Greek, and Oriental food, plus donuts, ice cream, and other sweet treats.

Showbiz Pizza, 10510 Metcalf, Overland Park, KS 66212, 648-4920. This popular family place has pizza, hot dogs, a salad bar and stage show, plus a game room with kiddie rides, ski ball, and videos. Birthday packages require advance reservations. (D)

Studebaker's/The Diner, I-435 and Metcalf, Overland Park, KS 66207, 345-1952. Not to be confused with Studebaker's adjacent Nightclub, the restaurant is designed in a '50s motif and features waitresses in ponytails and saddle shoes who do a choreographed "line dance" that kids and teens love to watch. The menu features children's dishes and old-fashioned ice cream sodas and malts and a D.J. entertains with funny musical routines. (D)

J.J. Tippin's Restaurant and Pie Pantry, 11005 Metcalf, Overland Park, KS 66207, 491-0926. With several locations around town, J.J. Tiippin's has made kids happy with 30 different whipped creamed, meringued and fruit-filled pies. They're just the thing to top off lunch or dinner. (D)

GOODIES

TCBY, several locations in Greater Kansas City including Glenwood Plaza at 91st and Metcalf, Overland Park, KS 66212, 341-0787. Check your phone book for other listings around town to taste some of the best tasting frozen yogurt around. (D)

T.J. Cinnamons, several locations in Greater Kansas City including 11528 W. 95th (95th St. and Quivira Rd.), Overland Park, KS 66218, 541-0444. Kids can't resist the delicious original gourmet cinnamon rolls served here and at several locations around town. (D)

Zarda Brothers Dairy, 10618 W. 63rd St., Shawnee, KS 66203, 631-5101. Zarda ice cream is a favorite with kids who love choosing their favorite flavor here. (D)

FAIRWAY AND PRAIRIE VILLAGE

BUSINESS AND COMMERCIAL TOURS

KMBZ/KMBR Radio, 4935 Belinder, Shawnee Mission, KS 66205, 236-9800. Children may tour the entire facility including the working newsroom, studios and computer systems. The friendly staff holds a question and answer period at the end. *Time Frame:* 15 minutes. *Ages:* 8 up. *Important to Know:* (I/R) (G/R) (No $) (B) ⚊

HISTORIC SITES AND MUSEUMS

Shawnee Methodist Mission and Indian Manual Labor School, 3403 W. 53rd St., Fairway, KS 66205, 262-0867. One of the earliest Indian missions established in pre-territorial Kansas (1839), this National Historical Landmark is open to tour. Youngsters seem most interested in the furnishings found inside the old-time classroom and dormitory for Indian children. *Time Frame;* 45 minutes. *Ages:* 3rd grade up. *Important to Know:* (I) (G/R) (No $) (B)

THE ARTS

Youth Symphony Assn. of Kansas City, Inc., 7645 Tomahawk, Prairie Village, KS 66208, 642-7141. Two ensembles comprised of the Youth Symphony and the Junior Youth Symphony perform in White Recital Hall in the Center for the Performing Arts on the UMKC campus at 4949 Cherry in midtown Kansas City, MO. The groups are open by audition. *Ages:* under 21. *Important to Know:* ($ to join; $ for performances)

PLAYING TOGETHER

Gymboree, 6529 High Drive, Shawnee Mission, KS 66208, 677-5880. Gymboree is an international play and movement program designed for parent/child interaction. The sessions, given at several Johnson County locations, emphasize natural play, socialization, and physical fitness. It's a good way to get quality time with your children. *Time Frame:* 45 minutes. *Ages:* 3 months to 5 years. *Important to Know:* (I/R) ($) (B)

THE GREAT OUTDOORS

Special Area Parks and Playgrounds

Phone or write the Johnson County Parks and Recreation Department (see Assistance, Overland Park, KS) for a complete listing of parks in your area.

Harmon Park, 7711 Delmar, Prairie Village, KS 66208, 381-6464. Adjacent to the Prairie Village Municipal Building and Community Center this complex has many indoor and outdoor activities for kids including swimming and tennis. Lessons are available. *Important to Know:* ($) (B) (D)

SPECIAL LIBRARY PROGRAMS

Parent/Child Learning Centers, Johnson County Libraries (Oak Park, Lackman, Corinth, Antioch, Cedar Roe), P.O. Box 2901, Shawnee Mission, KS 66201, 831-1550. (See Special Library Programs, Overland Park, KS.)

SPECIAL EVENTS CALENDAR

JUNE

Prairie Village Art and Crafts Show, Prairie Village Merchants Assn., 71st and Mission Rd., Prairie Village Shopping Center, Prairie village, KS 66208, 362-9668. The show features artists from around the area who display their work. Children have a special area where they can have a hands-on experience with a variety of art mediums. (No $)

GOODIES

Famous Amos Cookies and Ice Cream, 6978 Mission Rd. (Prairie Village Shopping Center), Prairie Village, KS 62608, 722-1297. Famous Amos cookies are sold here plus a variety of ice cream flavors and pizza. Fixings for children's birthday parties are a specialty.

Laura Little's Candies, 2100 W. 75th St., Prairie Village, KS 66208, 722-2226. This is the place to come for delicious fudge, chocolate suckers, caramel apples, popcorn, birthday cakes, and gummy items in the shapes of dinosaurs, tarantulas and (yuk!) rats, plus kid-sized ice cream bars.

SHAWNEE AND MERRIAM

ASSISTANCE

Convention Bureaus and Chambers of Commerce

Merriam Chamber of Commerce, 8600 W. 63rd St., Merriam, KS 66203, 236-6471.

Shawnee Chamber of Commerce, P.O. Box 3449, 10913 Shawnee Mission Pkwy., Shawnee, KS 66203, 631-6545.

Clubs and Organizations

Heart of America Council, Boy Scouts of America. (See Assistance, Kansas City, KS.)

Mid-Continent Council of Girl Scouts. (See Assistance, East of Plaza, Kansas City, MO.)

The Santa Fe Trail Council of Girl Scouts, Inc. (See Assistance, Kansas City, KS.)

Sunflower Council of Camp Fire, Inc., 12430 W. 62nd **Terrace, Shawnee, KS 66216, 631-6222.** Co-educational group activity programs for school-aged children stress self-reliance and decision-making skills in a fun, informal atmosphere. Resident and weekend camping programs teach youngsters how to enjoy the beauty of nature and preserve it for the future. Camp Fire self-reliance courses educate kids about the basics of safety, good citizenship skills, responsibility and assertiveness. *Ages:* K-12th Grade. *Important to Know:* (I) ($) (D)

YMCA Of Greater Kansas City. (See Clubs and Organizations, Midtown, Kansas City, MO.)

Special Assistance for the Disabled

Direction Service Center. (See Listing under Special Assistance for the Disabled, Independence, MO.) This organization publishes a pamphlet featuring summer programs for disabled children.

Johnson County Special Transportation, 6400 Carter, Merriam, KS 66203, 362-1111.

The Whole Person, Inc. (See Listing under Special Assistance for the Disabled, South of Plaza, Kansas City, MO.) This is a private not-for-profit organization for people with disabilities.

HISTORIC SITES AND MUSEUMS

Johnson County Historical Museum, 6305 Lackman Rd., Shawnee, KS 66217, 631-6709. The museum houses changing exhibits of interest to families. Ask about the hands-on history room for kids, complete with old-fashioned implements and machines. *Time Frame:* 30 minutes. *Ages:* 60 up. *Important to Know:* (I) (G) (No $) (B)

Old Shawnee Town, 3 blocks west of Nieman Rd. on 57th St., Shawnee, KS 66203, 268-8772. Operated by the Shawnee Historical Society, the museum is a replica of an 1890's town, complete with turn-of-the-century replicas and restored structures. Kids favorites are the old jail and school house. Pre-schoolers like the adjacent park that houses a play structure which resembles the town. *Time Frame:* 20 minutes minimum. *Ages:* pre-school up. *Important to Know:* (I) (G/R) (No $) (B)

THE ARTS

Theater in the Park, Shawnee Mission Park, 77th and Renner Rd., Johnson County Parks and Recreation, 6501 Antioch, Shawnee Mission, KS 66202, 831-3355. Musical productions, many of which are suitable for children, are held here and include such guests as the Kansas City Symphony. Bring your blankets, lawn chairs, and insect repellents and enjoy this outdoor summer entertainment. *Time Frame:* about 2 hours. *Ages:* all. *Important to Know:* (I) (G) ($) (B) (D)

SPORTS

Johnson County Parks and Recreation, 6501 Antioch, Shawnee Mission, KS 66202, 831-3355. Football, soccer, basketball, track, and tennis are just part of the seasonal sports programs offered by parks and recreation districts located throughout Johnson County. Parents can participate in scoring some events. Call for information on your area.

PLAYING TOGETHER

Shawnee Mission Park Trim Orienteering Course, 7900 Renner Rd., Shawnee, KS 66217, 631-5208, 831-3355. (See The Great Outdoors, this section.)

THE GREAT OUTDOORS

Special Programs and Exhibits

Shawnee Mission Park Trim Orienteering Course,
7900 Renner Rd., Shawnee, KS 66217, 631-5208, 831-3355.
The park features the first permanent "Trim" orienteering course in Kansas. Orienteering involves using a compass and special park map to find your way around the park. Kids and parents find this activity challenging and fun. *Ages:* 7-up. *Important to Know:* parents can purchase an information packet and map at the park office. (I) (G) (No $) (B)

Tomahawk Recreation Complex, 17501 Midland Dr., **Shawnee, KS 66218, 268-7252.** The complex has an 18-hole golf course, driving range, pro shop, lounge, and sports dome for athletic activities. There's also gymnastics for toddlers through teens and a swimming pool. *Ages:* pre-school up. *Important to Know:* (I/R) (G/R) ($) (B)

Special Area Parks and Playgrounds

There are many parks located in Johnson County. Most are equipped with picnic areas, ball fields, tennis courts, playgrounds, shelters, bathrooms and more. Phone or write the Johnson County Parks and Recreation (see Assistance, Overland Park, KS) for a complete listing of parks in your area. In the meantime here are a few of the larger ones:

Antioch Park, 6501 Antioch Rd., Merriam, KS 66202, 831-3355. The beautiful setting complete with fishing lakes, picnic shelters, an arboretum and rose garden makes this park a favorite. There's a play area called "Old Dodge Town" for kids that boasts unique structures for climbing. *Important to Know:* (I) (G) (No $) (B) (D)

Shawnee Mission Park, 7900 Renner Rd., Shawnee, KS 66217, 631-5208. This multi-use 1,250-acre park is the largest in Johnson County. It offers an 150-acre lake complete with boat marina and swimming beach with concessions. The visitors center provides a map of the area that outlines the playgrounds, hiking and horseback riding trails, remote controlled airplane field and orienteering course. *Important to Know:* (I) (G) (No $) (B) (D)

Summer Camping Programs

New Horizons Camp for Special Education Students, Rhein Benninghoven Elementary School, 6720 Caenen, Shawnee, KS. Write or phone Johnson County Parks and Recreation, 6501 Antioch, Shawnee Mission, KS 66202, 831-3355. This summer day camp features swimming, field trips, sports, games, fitness, arts and crafts, cooking and other special events for the physically and mentally disabled. *Ages:* 5 to 18. *Important to Know:* (I/R) ($) (B) (D)

SPECIAL LIBRARY PROGRAMS

Parent/Child Learning Centers, Johnson County Libraries (Oak Park, Lackman, Corinth, Antioch, Cedar Roe), P.O. Box 2901, Shawnee Mission, KS 66201, 831-1550. (See Special Library Programs, Overland Park, KS)

SPECIAL ACTIVITIES

Fun Services of Kansas City, 12119 Johnson Drive, Shawnee, KS 66216, 631-3717. This place sells fun stuff for all ages such as balloons, prizes, masks, costumes, toys, party supplies, wigs and more. They also rent equipment like booths and moonwalks as well as professional costumes for special occasions. *Ages:* all. *Important to Know:* (I) (G) ($) (B)

SPECIAL EVENTS CALENDAR

JUNE

Old Shawnee Days, Shawnee Chamber of Commerce and Shawnee Historical Society, Old Shawnee Town, 57th and Cody, Shawnee, KS 66203, 631-6545. This event celebrates the heritage of Shawnee, Kansas. There's plenty for kids including a children's parade, frog and turtle races, petting zoo, hot air balloon ride and a staged gunfight. (No $) (D)

DECEMBER

Pioneer Christmas, Shawnee Historical Society, Old Shawnee Town, 57th and Cody, Shawnee, KS 66203, 268-8772. The annual old-fashioned holiday event includes a Santa Claus, a Christmas-tree lighting ceremony, entertainment and prizes. (No $) (D)

FUN EATS

Poppa Z's Pizza, 12280 W. 63rd St., Shawnee, KS 66216, 268-8800 (also see location at 63rd St. and I-435). Aside from pizza, salad bar and soft drinks, the restaurant provides children's amusements such as kiddie rides, videos, and games, plus a playground for kids ages 2 to 5. (D)

LENEXA AND OLATHE

ASSISTANCE

Convention Bureaus and Chambers of Commerce

Lenexa Chamber of Commerce, 8700 Monrovia, Lenexa, KS 66215, 888-1414.

Lenexa Convention and Visitors Bureau, 11900 W. 87th St. Pkwy., Suite 115, Lenexa, KS 66215, 888-6570.

Olathe Area Chamber of Commerce, 128 S. Chestnut, P.O. Box 98, Olathe, KS 66061, 764-1050.

Special Assistance

Johnson County Information, 301A S. Clairborne, Olathe, KS 66062, 764-7007. This information phone answers questions about county government, services, and human service agency programs.

Johnson County Child Care Association, 5750 W. 95th St., Suite 140, Overland Park, KS 66207, 341-6200.

The Day Care Connection, 8931 W. 75th St., Overland Park, KS 66204, 962-2020.

Special Assistance for the Disabled

Johnson County Deaf Services Program, 301A S. Clairborne, Olathe, KS 66062, 764-7109. This is a hallmark program known throughout the country.

Johnson County Disability Awareness Program, 301A S. Clairborne, Olathe, KS 66062, 764-7007.

Transportation

Johnson County Transit, 9601 Alden, Lenexa, KS 66215, 541-8450.

BUSINESS AND COMMERCIAL TOURS

Johnson County Industrial Airport, Industrial Airport, KS 66031, 782-5335. The popular tour features an inside look at the U.S. Army Reserve Helicopter Unit. Kids are invited inside the largest helicopter, the CH-47, where they can sit in the pilot's seat and play with the controls. *Time Frame:* about 1 hour. *Ages:* pre-schoolers to teens. *Important to Know:* (G/R) (No $) (B) (D)

Olathe Daily News, 514 S. Kansas Ave., Olathe, KS 66061, 764-2211. Tours include a visit with a reporter or editor, and a look at various departments, computers, press room and more. *Time Frame:* 45 minutes. *Ages:* 1st grade up. *Important to Know:* (G/R) (No $) (B) (D)

Olathe Fire Station, Public Safety Bldg., 501 E. 56 Highway, Olathe, KS 66061, 782-4500. Children can tour the station, see the fire trucks and visit the fire fighters' quarters. Fire safety, prevention and survival techniques are stressed. *Time Frame:* 1 hour. *Ages:* 4 up. *Important to Know:* (G/R) (No $) (B) (D)

Olathe Police Dept., Public Safety Bldg., 501 E. 56 Highway, Olathe, KS 66061, 782-4500. This tour takes kids into the jail when unoccupied, and through a courtroom for a look through a 2-way mirror. They also get a glimpse of the polygraph machine. *Time Frame:* 30 minutes. *Ages:* 8 up. *Important to Know:* proper decorum a must. *Important to Know:* (G/R) (No $) (B) (D)

The Cookie Factory, Oak Park Mall, 11729 W. 95th St., Lenexa, KS 66214, 492-8188. (See Goodies, this section.)

HISTORIC SITES AND MUSEUMS

Ensor Historical Site and Park, 18995 183rd St., Olathe, KS 66062. Built in 1909 by the Marshall Ensor family, this former dairy farm now houses an outstanding display of early radio equipment including a complete ham station licensed in 1922. *Time Frame:* 20 minutes. *Ages:* 8 up. *Important to Know:* (I) (G/R) (No $) (B)

J. Mett Shippee Museum of American Indian Archeology, Sar-Ko-Par Park, 87th and Lackman Rd., Lenexa, Dept. of Parks and Recreation, 13420 Oak, Lenexa, KS 66215, 541-8592. Phone for the latest information on this new Lenexa museum. Here you'll find an important collection of prehistoric and early historic American Indian artifacts, primarily from the Kansas City region. *Time Frame:* 1 hour. *Ages:* K up. *Important to Know:* (I) (G/R) (B) (D)

Legler Barn Museum, 14907 W. 87th Pkwy., Lenexa, KS 66215, 492-0038. The museum contains artifacts pertaining to early Lenexa and Johnson County history. Of particular interest for kids is a railroad depot and caboose, old-fashioned school equipment, and a barbed-wire collection. There's also a playground on the premises. *Time Frame:* 15 minutes. *Ages:* all. *Important to Know:* (I) (G/R) (No $) (B) (D)

Mahaffie Farmstead and Stagecoach Stop, 1100 Old Kansas City Rd., Olathe, KS 66061, 782-6972. The farmstead marks the last remaining stagecoach stop along the Santa Fe Trail and the stone house and wood peg barn is listed on the National Register of Historic Places. Kids seem to find the chamber pots and old-fashioned mouse trap of particular interest. *Time Frame:* 30 minutes. *Ages:* 7 up. *Important to Know:* (I/R) (G/R) ($) (B)

THE ARTS

Olathe Community Theater Assn., 500 E. Loula, Olathe, KS 66061, 782-2990. The company performs works ranging from drama and comedy to musicals. Each June the theater puts on a children's production with open auditions for kids ages 8 to 12. They also have a Christmas variety show where they bring children from the audience onstage. *Ages:* toddlers up. *Important to Know:* (I/R) (G/R) ($) (B)

AMUSEMENTS

Fun Factory, Oak Park Mall, 1 W. 95th St., Lenexa, KS 66214, 492-3007. This huge indoor amusement center has several locations around town and features kiddie rides, video and pinball and arcade-style games. *Ages:* preschoolers up. *Important to Know:* (I) (G) ($) (B) (D-lower level, south door)

Galaxy Family Fun Center, 114 N. Clairborne, Olathe, KS 66062, 764-5676. The arcade features video and pinball games plus other games in which players test their skills for prizes. *Ages:* 8 up. *Important to Know:* (I) (G) ($) (B)

Grand Slam U.S.A., 8875 Rosehill Rd., Lenexa, KS 66215, 888-6961. This indoor complex features baseball and softball hitting ranges, a Slam Dunk basketball court and a slot-car raceway. Private and group lessons are available and yearly "camps" teach hitting, pitching and fielding. *Ages:* 4 up. *Important to Know:* (I) (G) ($) (B)

Smiley's Golf, 8201 Quivira Rd., Lenexa, KS 66215, 888-5355. In addition to twin miniature golf courses and game room, the complex features a "Jungle Land" complete with waterfalls and realistic animals, and an "Oriental Land" with a waterfall, miniature volcano, Tikki gods and a Buddha. Birthday party packages available. *Ages:* pre-school up. *Important to Know:* (I) (G/R) ($) (B)

PLAYING TOGETHER

"Imagination Station," Olathe Public Library, 201 E. Park, Olathe, KS 66061, 764-2259. (See Special Library Programs this section.)

SPORTS

Windaway Stables, 15315 W. 119th St., Olathe, KS 66062, 764-3888. The stable provides boarding and lessons. *Important to Know:* (I/R) (G/R) ($) (B) (D)

THE GREAT OUTDOORS

Special Area Parks and Playgrounds

There are many parks located in Johnson County. Most are equipped with picnic areas, ball fields, tennis courts, play-

grounds, shelters, bathrooms and more. Phone or write the Johnson County Park and Recreation Department (see Assistance, Overland Park, KS.) for a complete listing of parts in your area. In the meantime here are a few of the larger ones:

Ernie Miller Park, 909 N. K-7 Highway at 131st St., Olathe, KS 66061, 764-7759. (Also see Nature Sanctuaries.) The 113-acre park features a nature center, nature study areas and a handicapped-accessible nature trail. There is year-around interpretive programming for all ages. *Important to Know:* (I) (G) ($) (B) (D)

Heritage Park, 16050 Pflumm Rd., Olathe, KS 66062, 782-7625. A 45-acre lake with marina features pedal boats, windsurfer rentals and concessions. There are children's playgrounds in this 1,160-acre park which is close to the Deanna Rose Memorial Farmstead (See Nature Sanctuaries, Overland Park, KS.) Jogging and horseback riding areas, fishing and sports fields round out the offerings. *Important to Know:* (I) (G) ($ for rental) (B)

Mill Creek Streamway Park, 114th to 119th St., W. of Ridgeview Rd., Olathe, KS 66061, 831-3355. Biking, hiking, jogging, canoeing, horseback riding and more can be enjoyed along the miles of open spaces provided here. Important to Know: (I) (G) (No $) (B)

Nature Sanctuaries

Prairie Center, 26325 W. 135th St., Olathe, KS 66061, 677-3326. The 300 acres of tallgrass prairie include a lake and ponds, plus hiking and self-guided nature trails, and a variety of native midwestern plants and animals. One of two nature centers involved in the Outdoor Education Laboratory program (see Outdoor Education, Overland Park, KS) The area holds special programs year-around, including family-oriented speakers and cross-country skiing. *Ages:* all. *Important to Know:* (I) (G/R) ($ for some programs) (B)

Ernie Miller Park and Nature Center, 9909 N. K-7 Highway at 131st St., Olathe, KS 66061, 764-7759. The center provides many habitat trails, nature displays, a diorama and exhibits which interpret the ecology of the park throughout the seasons. There are varied educational programs offered throughout the year and summer evening programs are held at the outdoor amphitheater. The center's newsletter keeps you updated on events. *Ages:* all. *Important to Know:* (I) (G) (No $) (B) (D)

SPECIAL LIBRARY PROGRAMS

"Imagination Station," Olathe Public Library, 201 E. Park, Olathe, KS 66061, 764-2259. This parent/child program features tabletop activities designed to enhance reading readiness. Sponsored by the Olathe Junior Service League, the theme-oriented program changes monthly during the school year. The stimulating activities involve shapes, colors, numbers, animals and more. Parents can get involved by reading instructions, helping in the tasks and sharing time with their children. *Ages:* pre-schoolers up. *Important to Know:* (I) (No $) (B) (D)

SPECIAL EVENTS CALENDAR

APRIL

Spring Prairie Festival, Prairie Center, 26325 W. 135th St., Olathe, KS 66061, 677-3326. Tours and exhibits are of special interest. *Important to Know:* ($)

JULY

Bullwhacker Days, City of Olathe, Mahaffie Farmstead, 1100 Kansas City Rd., Olathe, KS 66061, 782-6972. Bullwhacker Days celebrates the history of the Mahaffie Farmstead and stagecoach stop along the Santa Fe Trail. Festivities include old-time crafts, entertainment, food and games. Kids like the covered wagon rides and the chance to lock their parents up in the jail. *Important to Know:* (No $)

Lenexa Community Days, City of Lenexa, Santa Fe and Pflumm, Lenexa, KS 66215, 541-8592. The annual event celebrates the Independence Day with the Lenexa State Barbecue Contest, a street fair, 10 K run, Miss Lenexa contest for young women ages 14 to 18, live entertainment, food and crafts. There's a kid's pet show, a petting zoo, carnival booths and a teen event. *Important to Know:* (No $)

Lenexa Spinach Festival, City of Lenexa, Sar-Ko-Par Park, 87th and Lackman Rd., 66215, 541-8592. The yearly festival commemorates the '30s when the city was known as the "spinach capital of the world," due to a drought in the rest of the country. There's plenty of entertainment, an arts and crafts fair and games for kids of all ages. Children like the tricycle parade and the visit by Popeye. *Important to Know:* (No $)

SEPTEMBER

Fall Rendezvous, Prairie Center, 26325 W. 135th St., Olathe, KS 66061, 677-3326. Music, exhibits and tours are part of the fun. *Important to Know:* ($)

Old Settlers Celebration, Johnson County Old Settlers, downtown Olathe at Kansas and Santa Fe Sts., Olathe, KS 66061, 764-1050. The two-day event commemorates Johnson County's history. Festivities include a parade, entertainment, food, contests, a craft fair, and more. There's a kiddie parade for children. *Important to Know:* (No $) (D)

DECEMBER

Victorian Christmas Open House, The Mahaffie Farmstead/City of Olathe, 1100 Kansas City Rd., Olathe, KS 66061, 782-6972. The home and farmstead is decorated in the Victorian style for the holidays. While parents tour the home, children are invited to the basement workshops to make tin-punched and paper ornaments. *Important to Know:* ($)

FUN EATS

Fast Food Havens, 87th/Santa Fe Strip between Lenexa and Overland Park, KS. Burgers, fried chicken, tacos—you name it. It's all here.

Fast Food Havens, Santa Fe Drive ("The Strip"), Olathe, **KS.** Here's a smorgasbord of fast food places. Drive-throughs are popular, with steak houses running a close second.

Pizza Paddle Pizza and Ice Cream Parlors, 9556 **Quivira Rd., Lenexa, KS 66215, 888-5631.** The pizza parlor offers a birthday party package complete with pizza, soft drinks, candy, party hats, ice cream and cake.

GOODIES

The Cookie Factory, Oak Park Mall, 11729 W. 95th St., **Lenexa, KS 66214, 492-8188.** The store bakes and decorates cookies of all shapes and sizes. Tours are available Monday through Wednesday with advance notice. Kids can watch their favorite cookie cakes being made and, as a bonus, get to eat it after the demonstration.

BUCYRUS AND LOUISBURG

The following family-oriented attractions are close enough to the Greater Kansas City Metro area to merit inclusion here:

SPORTS

Hunter's Vale Equestrian Center, 207th and Quivira, **Bucyrus, KS 66013, 764-7440.** Group and private lessons, clinics and summer camp are offered for students as well as horse boarding and training. *Ages:* 4 up. *Important to Know:* (I/R) (G/R) ($) (B)

SPECIAL ACTIVITIES

Louisburg Cider Mill, South on U.S. 69 to K-68 and west 4 miles, Louisburg, KS 66053, 913-837-5202. Over 20,000 pounds of apples are pressed here during apple season. Children love to watch the apple-pressing and donut-making. They can also glimpse cider jugs being filled and apple butter being made. Tours are available in fall. Make a day of it: visit the Cider Mill in the afternoon, followed by dinner at nearby Blair House, and stargazing at Powell Observatory. *Important to Know:* (I) (G/R) (No $ for tours) (B) (D)

Powell Observatory, just off 263rd St. and U.S. 69, 3 miles N.W. of Louisburg, KS, c/o Astronomical Society of Kansas City, P.O. Box 400, Blue Springs, MO 64015, 373-2614. Run by the Astronomical Society of Kansas City, Powell Observatory houses a 30-inch, computer-controlled telescope for public viewing of the night skies from May to October. Located in Lewis-Young Park, the facility has a heated classroom with bathrooms attached to the 20-foot domed observatory where star observing parties are held twice a month. Members happily share their out-of-this-world knowledge with newcomers. There is also a Junior

Astronomers Group for kids 10 to 17. *Important to Know:* kids should be at least 36" tall to use the big scope and old enough to understand what they're seeing. (I/R) (G/) (donation) (B)

FUN EATS

Blair House, 5th and Metcalf, Louisburg, KS 66053, 913-837-4419. In business for 20 years, this family-style restaurant features a smorgasbord featuring home-cooking that includes fried chicken, spaghetti, vegetables, salads, and dessert. Special prices for kids under 10; children under 2 are free.

GARDNER AND EDGERTON

HISTORIC SITES AND MUSEUMS

Lanesfield School Museum, 18745 South Dillie, Edgerton, KS 66021, 913-631-6709. The oldest one-room schoolhouse in the area was built in 1869 and was a mail stop along the Old Santa Fe Trail. Restored as a "living history" classroom, it's open to tour. Phone for updated information.

SPECIAL EVENTS

Johnson County Fair, Johnson County Fair Board Committee, Johnson County Fairground, Gardner, KS 66030, 913-884-8860. The fair, which was started in 1922, features contests, 4-H projects and livestock exhibits. Carnival rides, a rodeo, demolition derby, petting area and dog show are part of the fun. *Important to Know:* (No $)

WYANDOTTE COUNTY, KANSAS

KANSAS CITY, KANSAS, BONNER SPRINGS, AND EDWARDSVILLE

KEY: (I) individual tours, no reservations needed; (I/R) individual tours, reservations needed; (G) group tours, no reservations needed; (G/R) group tours, reservations needed; ($) fee; (No $) no fee; (B) bathrooms; (No B) no bathrooms; (D) some accommodations for the disabled.

KANSAS CITY, KANSAS

ASSISTANCE

Convention Bureaus and Chambers of Commerce

Kansas City, Kansas, Convention Bureau, 636 Minnesota, P.O. Box 171517, Kansas City, KS 66117, 321-5800.

Kansas City, Kansas Chamber of Commerce, 729 Minnesota, Kansas City, KS 66101, 371-3070.

Clubs and Organizations

Sunflower Council of Camp Fire, Inc. (See Assistance, Shawnee, KS, Johnson County.)

Heart of America Council, Boy Scouts of America, Two Gateway Center, 400 State Ave., Kansas City, KS 66101, 321-5151. This organization helps boys develop into young men who are confident, poised and responsible. Group activities stress self-assurance, teamwork and leadership skills. Family and neighborhood-centered programs are designed to be a natural extension of home, church and school. Troop and patrol-centered agendas build and foster lifetime skills. Unique itineraries for older boys provide team activities, career and lifetime avocational opportunities through business partnerships. Day, resident, handicap, specialty, and honor camps and national summer outdoor programs foster a love of outdoors and encourage resourcefulness. *Ages:* 1st grade through age 20. *Important to Know:* (I) ($) (D)

The Santa Fe Trail Council of Girl Scouts, Inc., 7620 State Avenue, Kansas City, KS 66112, 334-2020. An extension of the largest girl's organization in the world, the Santa Fe Trail Council provides opportunities and activities that develop skills in decision-making, leadership, career development, environmental awareness and recreation. Developing self-potential and high ethical values are stressed. Activities are centered around out-of-doors camping and sports, health and well-being, learning about people, career exploration, and the arts. The groups are headed by an adult leader who acts as a role model. *Ages:* K-12th grade. *Important to Know:* (I) ($) (D)

YMCA

YMCA Youth Extension, 2940 N. 17th St., Kansas City, KS 66104, 371-5746; Central Branch: 900 N. 8th St., Kansas City, KS 66101, 371-4400; West Branch: 7340 State Avenue, Kansas City, KS 66112, 299-1242; YMCA, 1017 N. 6th St., Kansas City, KS 66101, 371-1105. These organizations have an abundance of sports and cultural programs for kids, plus day camps, child care, and other offerings.

Special Assistance for the Disabled

Direction Service Center. (See Listing under Special Assistance for the Disabled, Independence, MO.) This organization publishes a pamphlet featuring summer programs for children with disabilities.

Kansas City, Kansas, Parks and Recreation. (See Summer Camping Programs, The Great Outdoors.)

The Whole Person, Inc. (See Listing under Special Assistance for the Disabled, South of Plaza, Kansas City, MO.) This is a private not-for-profit organization for people with disabilities.

Transportation

The Bus, 701 N. 7th St., Kansas City, KS 66102, 371-6402. If you have questions about the mini-buses that serve Wyandotte County, just call and they'll send you a schedule. (D)

Parks and Recreation Departments

Kansas City, Kansas, Sports and Program Hotline, 24 Hours, 342-0168. (Also see Parks and Recreation, The Great Outdoors.)

Wyandotte County Parks, 3488 West Drive, Kansas City, KS 66109, 299-0550.

BUSINESS AND COMMERCIAL TOURS

Associated Grocers, Inc., 5000 Kansas Ave., Kansas City, KS 66106, 321-1313, Ext. 314. Kids can tour this distribution facility where they'll see meat and produce areas and watch railroad cars full of food being unloaded. *Time Frame:* 1 hour. *Ages:* 8 up. *Important to Know:* children should wear light jackets for visiting the frozen food department. (G/R) (No $) (B)

Board of Public Utilities—Electric Plant, 55th and Missouri River, Kansas City, KS 66101, 573-9173. Children can visit the control room which is all lit up and look at the enormous equipment that generates electricity. *Time Frame:* 1 hour. *Ages:* 10 up. *Important to Know:* wear flat shoes (for grids) and dark clothes (for dust). Tours restricted to service area residents. (G/R) (No $) (B)

Board of Public Utilities—Water Purification Plant, 10th St. and Missouri River, Kansas City, KS 66101, 573-9173. Children learn about the purification process from river to tap water. They'll see glass containers of water samples at various stages and watch the rapid sand filter at work. *Time Frame:* 1 hour. *Ages:* 3rd grade up. *Important to Know:* wear sensible clothing and shoes. Tours restricted to service area residents. (G/R) (No $) (B)

El Taquito, 640 Reynolds, Kansas City, KS 66101, 371-0452. Children can tour this tortilla plant where they'll learn how and where corn for tortillas is stored and get a behind-the-scenes look at how tortillas are made. *Time Frame:* 30 minutes. *Ages:* 3 up. *Important to Know:* (I/R) (G/R) (No $) (B)

Fresh Start Bakeries, 530 S. 65th St., Kansas City, KS 66111, 287-6300. This bakery bakes the hamburger buns for the McDonald's restaurants. It's totally automated and kids follow the making and baking process and then sample the results. *Time Frame:* 45 minutes. *Ages:* 1st grade up. *Important to Know:* no cameras allowed. Wear tennis shoes. Hairnets provided. (G/R) (No $) (B)

General Motors, 3201 Fairfax Trafficway, Kansas City, KS 66115, 573-7115. The tour covers all aspects of auto assembling and finishing, except painting. Of special interest: the robot auto body assembing. *Time Frame:* 1 hour. *Ages:* 8 up. *Important to Know:* no cameras allowed. (G/R) (No $) (B)

Kansas City, Kansas, Municipal Office Building, 701 N. 7th St., Kansas City, KS 66101, 573-6225. The tour covers the courts, the Police Department's I.D. unit, line-up and communications rooms and holding tank, if empty. Specific requests can net you a discussion of city govern-

ment and a meeting with the Mayor. *Time Frame:* 1 hour. *Ages:* 9 up. *Important to Know:* (G/R) (No $) (B)

Wyandotte County Court House, 710 N. 7th St., **Kansas City, KS 66101, 573-2940.** The court house tour takes in the sheriff's office with its cameras and monitors, court rooms, treasurer's office where car tags are purchased and anything else of group interest. *Time Frame:* 1 hour. *Ages:* pre-school up. *Important to Know:* (G/R) (No $) (B)

HISTORIC SITES AND MUSEUMS

Grinter Place, 1420 S. 78th St., Kansas City, KS 66111, **299-0373.** The oldest remaining private dwelling in Wyandotte County, the home was built in 1857 by Moses Grinter who operated the first ferry on the Kansas River. Kids can tour the structure, visit the children's room and learn about survival techniques, pioneer living and Indian heritage. *Time Frame:* 30 minutes. *Ages:* 7 up. *Important to Know:* (I) (G/R) (No $) (B)

Huron Indian Cemetery, 6th to 7th Sts., Minnesota to Ann Sts., Kansas City, KS 66101. Established in 1843, the cemetery was saved from demolition by three Indian sisters led by Lyda Conley. On her tombstone Helena "Floating Voice" Conley put a curse on anyone who would defile the land. Although it sits in a business district, the cemetery provides a lovely setting for a quiet walk and contains many Indian graves. It's adjacent to the Kansas City, Kansas, Public Library and Huron Rose Garden. *Important to Know:* (I) (G) (No $) (No B)

Kansas Children's Museum, 1100 State Ave., Kansas City, KS 66102, 321-4263. The museum provides hands-on learning about the history and culture, science and technology, and the arts pertaining to the state of Kansas. Children can blow bubbles, trade rocks, do science experiments, try on pioneer clothing and generally have a great time learning about new things. The museum's traveling exhibits also bring in exciting programs of interest to kids. *Time Frame:* 2 hours. *Ages:* all. *Important to Know:* (I) (G/R) ($) (B)

Worth a Drive-by:

Kansas City, Kansas, has some unusual historic sites that might be of interest for children. They include:

John Brown Statue, 27th and Sewell. Dedicated in 1911, this marble statue was the first U.S. memorial erected to the famed abolitionist.

The Argentine Steps, 13th St. at Ruby Ave. Nothing could be more contrary to the image of flat Kansas than this street, so steep it had to be built as steps.

Rosedale World War I Memorial Arch in Mt. Marty Park, above the intersection of 7th and Southwest Blvd. Patterned after the Arc de Triomphe in Paris, it commemorates the 42nd or "Rainbow" Division which was the first American combat unit to arrive in France.

Fire Station #9, 14th St. and Wilson Blvd. Now a neighborhood center, the building has firemen gargoyles on the corners of the structure.

Sauer "Castle," 945 Shawnee Dr. Built at a cost of over $20,000 in 1871, the Italianate Villa-style home overlooks the Kansas River. It's supposedly haunted. No tours.

THE ARTS

Kansas City, Kansas, holds a bonanza of ethnic and cultural arts activities for children. Here's a sampling:

Aidas Lithuanian Dancers, 1731 N. 78th Terr., Kansas City, KS 66112, 299-1453. These Lithuanian dancers perform at festivals and schools entertaining children with lively dances and colorful costumes. *Time Frame:* performances run about 30 minutes. *Ages:* all. *Important to Know:* (G/R) ($ depends on event)

Creative Experiences, Inc., 1721 N. 79th St., Kansas City, KS 66102, 334-3034. Qualified instructors stimulate children's creativity with classes in art, music, drama, science and other areas of education. *Time Frame:* about 1 hour. *Ages:* 2 to 14. *Important to Know:* (I/R) ($) (B)

FairyTale Productions, Inc., 2101 Washington Blvd., Kansas City, KS 66102, 888-6650. The non-profit group stages elaborate musical productions of classic fairytales for kids. Each play has multiple scenery changes, special effects, costumes, and original music. All shows are given in the historic Granada Theatre where an open courtyard enhances the performance. There is also a huge pipe organ that provides music and special sound effects. *Time Frame:* 1 hour. *Ages:* pre-school to 4th grade. *Important to Know:* (I/R) (G/R) ($) (B) (D)

Granada Theatre, 1015 Minnesota, Kansas City, KS 66101, 621-7177. Built in 1928, this restored historic theater houses a performing arts center that offers films, concerts and children's plays (See FairyTale Productions, this section.) It also holds a rare theater pipe organ played during performances. *Time Frame:* about 2 hours. *Ages:* all. *Important to Know:* (I/R) (G/R) ($) (B)

Junior League of Kansas City, Kansas, Inc., P.O. Box 2485, Kansas City, KS 66110, 371-2303. The League stages entertaining productions of plays such as "Winnie the Pooh" and the "Wizard of Oz" for Kansas City, Kansas, kids. The costumes, music and staging are impressive for chldren. *Time Frame:* 1 hour. *Ages:* K to 6th grade. *Important to Know:* (G/R) (No $) (B) (D)

Kansas City Jazz Quintet, **947 Minnesota, Kansas City, KS 66101, 371-4157.** The Quintet's Young Audience-sponsored jazz concerts for area schools are geared to the age of the kids. Different instruments are introduced during the show. *Time Frame:* 45 minutes. *Ages:* pre-school up. *Important to Know:* (G/R) (Sliding $)

Kaw Valley Arts Council Gallery, **753 State Avenue, Suite 101, Kansas City, KS 66101, 371-0024.** This gallery displays a wide variety of art from paintings and photography to sculpture and fiber art. During Youth Arts Month (See Special Events) the artwork of area students is shown here. *Time Frame:* 15 minutes. *Ages:* all. *Important to Know:* (I) (G) (No $) (No B)

Kansas City, Kansas, Public Libraries, **625 Minnesota, Kansas City, KS 66101, 621-3073.** (Also see Special Library Programs, this section.) The Main Library and its West Wyandotte and Argentine branches hold different art displays, from paintings and fiber art to ceramics, artifacts and sculpture. There are hand-out materials to share with the kids. The library also rents books that pertain to the display. An annual juried art show sponsored by The Kaw Valley Arts Council is part of the program. *Time Frame:* 15 minutes or more. *Ages:* particularly suited for 4th to 8th graders. *Important to Know:* (I) (G) (No $) (B) (D)

M.C. Players, **510 N. 13th St., No. 5, Kansas City, KS 66102, 321-8427.** Talented performers from the community are part of this theatrical group that produces original plays written by its members. The company also holds workshops for children on pantomime, improvisation, and stage production. *Time Frame:* workshops are 40 minutes. *Ages:* 11 to 17. *Important to Know:* (I/R) (G/R) (No $) (B) (D)

Pipes of Clanna Eireann, in care of Loren Taylor, City Hall, 701 N. 7th St., Kansas City, KS 66101, 573-6195. The group gives Irish Heritage concerts called *Ceili* using traditional bagpipes and drums. You can see them at the annual St. Patrick's Day Parade and various other events. Kids love listening to the unusual instruments. Phone the group for more information on Irish dancing, song, spoken word and poetry. *Important to Know:* the group gives free drum and bagpipe lessons to children ages 10 to 12.

Rose Marie's Fiesta Mexicana, 3401 State Ave., Kansas City, KS 66102, 281-1352. Traditional Mexican dances are part of the repertoire of this local dance troupe that performs throughout the year at civic and social events and in public schools. Children love the colorful costumes and the history behind this educational and enjoyable cultural experience. Kids as young as 10 years old may audition for the group. *Time Frame:* 1½ hours. *Ages:* all. *Important to Know:* ($)

Serbian Folklore Group Dancers Delije, St. Michael Orthodox Church, 310 N. 72nd, Kansas City, KS 66112, 788-5845. National Serbian folk ballet is the focus of this teenage through 7th grade with guest performances by Theatre for civic functions, weddings and special occasions. Young children like the colorful costumes and dancing. There is also a junior group that performs made up of kids ages 6 to 11. *Time Frame:* 20-45 minutes. *Ages:* all. *Important to Know.* (No $)

Strawberry Hill Croatian Folk Ensemble, 2948 N. 70th St., Kansas City, KS 66109, 299-4795. This ensemble, consisting of young Croatian dancers and musicians, performs at area festivals and civic group events. The group's authentic vibrant costumes and music delights young and old alike. *Time Frame:* 45 minutes. *Ages:* all. *Important to Know:* ($)

Susan Warden Dancers, 618 Orient Dr., Kansas City, KS 66102, 371-2497. This modern dance company tours regionally in concert. It also teaches modern dance classes for kids and gives lecture-demonstration workshops featuring audience participation. *Time Frame:* 45 minute workshops; performances run 1½ hours. *Ages:* K to high school. *Important to Know:* the group requesting the workshop provides the space where it's held. ($)

St. John's Tamburitzans, St. John The Baptist Church, **4th and Barnett, Kansas City, KS 66101, 371-0627.** Comprised of 4th grade to high school students, the group performs Croatian music and dancing at year-around concerts and festivals. Led by musical director, Don Lipovac, the company's Slavic and Balkan dances bring a taste of European culture to Kansas City kids who find the costumes and dancing fun to watch. *Time Frame:* their annual concert is 2 hours. *Ages:* all. *Important to Know:* phone for updated concert information. ($)

Wyandotte Players, 7250 State Avenue, Kansas City, KS **66112, 596-9690.** This theatrical company puts on plays suitable for children. Many of the productions, given at the Kansas City, Kansas, Community College, are popular enough that parents could review the story line with kids before attending to enhance their understanding. Also on the college campus: a Lyceum Series for kids pre-school through 7th grade with guest performances by Theater for Young America and others. *Time Frame:* 1½ hours. *Ages:* pre-school up. *Important to Know:* (I/R) (G/R) ($) (B)

AMUSEMENTS

Fun Factory, Indian Springs Mall, 4601 State Ave., Kansas City, KS 66102, 596-2222. This fun center/arcade has games and rides for pre-schoolers. *Ages:* all. *Important to Know:* (I) (G) ($) (No B)

KCQ Family Billiards, 7540 Leavenworth Rd., Kansas City, KS 66109, 299-0383. Pool tables, snooker and a video room are available for parents and children. *Ages:* all. *Important to Know:* (I) (G) ($) (B)

Lyons Miniature Golf Course, 7650 State Ave., Kansas City, KS 66112, 334-3805. This 36-hole course is varied enough to keep kids interested. *Ages:* 5 up. *Important to Know:* (I) (G) ($) (B)

SPORTS

Kansas City, Kansas, Parks and Recreation Community Centers, 75 S. 23rd St., Kansas City, KS 66102, 371-4166. Parks and Recreation has several family-oriented facilities in the area that offer a wide variety of sports and outdoor activities for children. These include the Argentine, Armourdale, Bell, Bethany, Eisenhower, John F. Kennedy, Kensington and Parkwood Recreation Centers. For more information call the number listed above. Indoor summer swimming lessons are held at local area high schools. *Important to Know:* (I/R) (G/R) ($) (B)

Weekend Recreation Kit, Kansas City, Kansas, Parks and Recreation, 75 S. 23rd St., Kansas City, KS 66102, 371-4166. Need sports equipment for a summer picnic or party? A security deposit nets you a special "kit" good for two days that includes bat, ball, bases, volleyball, net, horseshoes and stakes. First come, first served.

Summer Playground Program, Kansas City, Kansas, Parks and Recreation, 75 S. 23rd St., Kansas City, KS 66102, 371-4166. The program includes classes in karate, basketball, tennis, swimming and more. (Also see Special Area Parks and Playgrounds, The Great Outdoors.) *Time Frame:* June/July. *Ages:* 8 to 12. *Important to Know:* (I) ($) (B)

Youth Softball Program and Youth Basketball Program, Kansas City, Kansas, Parks and Recreation, 75 S. 23rd St., Kansas City, KS 66102, 371-4166. Seasonal sessions are offered to kids who want to acquire skills in these team sports. Volleyball and karate classes are also held in winter. *Ages:* 4 to high school. *Important to Know:* (I) ($) (B)

Southern Wyandotte County Sports Association, P.O. Box 6195, Kansas City, KS 66106, 722-1561. The association helps children learn the fundamentals of baseball, softball and soccer, with an emphasis on good sportsmanship. Parents are encouraged to be coaches, managers and sponsors. *Ages:* 4 to 18. *Important to Know:* (I) ($)

Liondotte Baseball League, Inc., P.O. Box 4011, Kansas City, KS 66104, 299-0286. Kids learn the fundamentals of baseball and participate in every game as long as they have attended practice and paid their fees. Good sportsmanship and team cooperation are part of the learning experience. Parents are invited to become managers, coaches and sponsors. *Ages:* 5 to 14. *Important to Know:* The American Legion Posts sponsor baseball teams for kids 15 and up. (I) ($)

3 & 2 Baseball of Kansas, Inc., 5301 Parallel, Kansas City, KS 66110, 287-9739. This league, which covers both Johnson County and Missouri, has over 500 youths in its

program. Team spirit and good sportsmanship are "musts" for kids who want to learn the game. Parents can be coaches, managers and sponsors: *Ages:* 8 to 19. *Important to Know:* (I) ($)

Kansas City Beach Club, 5211 Parallel, Kansas City, KS 66104, 287-7070. This private swimming pool is for members only. *Ages:* all. *Important to Know:* (I) (G) ($) (B)

Parkwood Swimming Pool, 950 Quindaro, Kansas City, KS 66101, 371-0722. This public swimming pool is open to everyone. Phone for more information on group and evening reservations. *Ages:* all. *Important to Know:* (I) (G/R) ($) (B)

Wyandotte County Sports Association, 10100 Leavenworth Rd., Kansas City, KS 66109, 299-9197. The association has a wide array of sports for youth, from basketball, football and golf to softball. Kids enjoy learning and playing on the teams and gain coordination and good sportsmanship as a result. Parents can be managers and coaches. *Ages:* 5 to 18. *Important to Know:* (I) ($) (B)

Turner Recreation Commission, 1800 S. 55th St., Kansas City, KS 66106, 375-9626, 287-7500. The commission offers sports for kids including volleyball, soccer, football, hunter safety, gymnastics, basketball, wrestling, track, baseball and softball. There's also a summer arts and music session, coordinated with the Turner District Summer School Program. Phone for fees, schedules, and information.

YMCA (see Assistance, this section.)

THE GREAT OUTDOORS

Special Area Parks and Playgrounds

Summer Playground Program, Kansas City, Kansas, Parks and Recreation, 75 S. 23rd St., Kansas City, KS 66102, 371-4166. The program keeps kids occupied with classes in karate, tennis, basketball and swimming, plus dance, arts and crafts, and music. Parks and Recreation also provides a special Day Camp for the mentally disabled. *Time Frame:* June/July day-long sessions. *Ages:* 6 to 15. *Important to Know:* (I) ($) (B) (D)

Summer Wading Pools, Kansas City, Kansas, Parks and Recreation, 75 S. 23rd St., Kansas City, KS 66102, 371-4166. Supervised wading pools can be found at the following parks: Edgerton, 3rd and Edgerton Sts.; Clopper, 33rd and

Powell Sts.; Quindaro, 34th and Sewell Sts. *Ages:* 3 to 12. *Important to Know:* (I) (No $) (B)

Big Eleven Lake, 11th St. between State and Minnesota Aves., Kansas City, KS 66102, 371-4166. This small fishing lake in downtown Kansas City, KS, is located close to the Kansas Children's Museum. Kids can bait their hooks and drop a line in any time and take home their catch in time for dinner. Parents and grandparents can share important time here with the youngsters. *Important to Know:* no license needed for kids under 16.

Wyandotte County Parks and Recreation, 3488 W. Dr. (91st and Leavenworth Rd.), Kansas City, KS 66109, 299-0550. *Parks and Recreation manages the following parks:*

Wyandotte County Lake Park, 91st and Leavenworth Rd., Kansas City, KS 66109, 299-0550. There's a special kid's fishing hole stocked with channel catfish who'll bite at anything. Children can see waterfowl, deer and other wildlife, and feed Canadian geese here in winter. There's something of interest here for all, including boat rental, a playground and a model train for kids to ride the second Saturday of every month. Also of note: the Korea and Vietnam War Memorial located at the lake entrance. *Important to Know:* ($ for boat rental and fishing license) (D—boat dock ramp)

Wyandotte County Park, 126th and State Ave. in Bonner Springs, KS, 299-0550. (See Special Area Parks and Playgrounds, Bonner Springs, KS.)

Wyandotte County Pierson Park, 1800 S. 55th St., Kansas City, KS 66106, 299-0550. There's a fishing lake, tennis courts, playgrounds, shelters and a community building.

Outdoor Education Programs

Kansas City, Kansas, Community College Nature Trail, 7250 State Ave., Kansas City, KS 66112, 334-1100. The two-mile trail is marked with signs identifying trees, plants and other flora. Aside from holding the largest Burr Oak in

Kansas, the trail is an excellent place for birding and seeing small mammals, screech owls, and deer. Trail guides are available from the college fieldhouse or science division. Open all year, the trail is particularly beautiful after a snow. *Ages:* all. *Important to Know:* (I) (G/R) (No $) (B on campus)

Outdoor Fishing Derby, Westgate Bank Bldg., 6000 Leavenworth Rd., Kansas City, KS 66104, 788-3988. The Kansas Fish and Game Commission, Wyandotte County Park Board and Leavenworth Rd. Assn. hold a half-day Saturday fishing clinic in June to teach kids about fishing and sportsmanship. There are prizes for the biggest and smallest catch. The fun outdoor event is held at Wyandotte County Lake. *Ages:* 15 and under. *Important to Know:* Wyandotte County residents only. (I/R) (No $) (B)

Summer Camping Programs

Indian Day Camp, Wyandotte County Fairgrounds, 98th St. between State and Parallel Aves., Kansas City, KS 66111, 299-9300. Wyandotte County's rich Indian heritage has led to this unusual program where children get to spend a day as the Indians did. The kids gather in tepees to study the daily lives of these Native American settlers. They are given an Indian name and learn about sand painting, totem building, bead work, leathercraft, and cooking. Buffalo burgers might be served at lunch. *Time Frame:* one day. *Ages:* 5 to 10. *Important to Know:* registration is open to all, but Wyandotte County residents have preference. (I/R) ($) (B) (D)

Kansas City, Kansas, Parks and Recreation, 75 S. 23rd St., Kansas City, KS 66102, 371-4166. Parks and Recreation holds a summer day camp for mentally disabled kids at City Park Pavilion in June and July. Activities include arts and crafts, sports, field trips, swimming and more. Bus service is available. *Ages:* 5 to 20. *Important to Know:* (I/R) (No $) (B) (D)

Space Camp, Wyandotte County Fairgrounds, 98th St. between State and Parallel Ave., Kansas City, KS 66111, 299-9300. This one-day camp gives kids an out-of-this-world learning experience. Space games, rocket building, gravity experiments, astronomy and physics are part of the educational fun. Lunch consists of "space food." *Time Frame:* one day. *Ages:* 9 to 12. *Important to Know:* open registration, but Wyandotte County residents have preference. (I/R) ($) (B) (D)

SPECIAL LIBRARY PROGRAMS

Kansas City, Kansas, Public Libraries, 625 Minnesota, **Kansas City, KS 66101, 621-3073.** The Main Library and its West Wyandotte and Argentine branches offer summer and after-school activities for kids that include stories, games, arts and crafts, films and nature study. *Time Frame:* varies. *Ages:* 1st to 6th grade. *Important to Know:* (I/R) (No $) (B) (D)

ENTERTAINING PEOPLE

Cleo the Clown and Magician, 2124 N. 56th Terr., **Kansas City, KS 66104, 287-5268.** Any would-be clowns in your family? Cleo Thomann, as president of Clowns of America, holds meetings every month. Members include children as young as 10. As a home entertainer, Thomann arrives in a business suit and, in front of his young audience, proceeds to put on his make-up and costume. Thomann goes on to entertain the kids with magic and silly tricks and uses the tykes as helpers in the act. *Time Frame:* 45 minutes. *Ages:* pre-schoolers up. *Important to Know:* (G/R) ($)

SPECIAL ACTIVITIES

Argentine Community Center, 2810 Metropolitan **Ave., Kansas City, KS 66106, 432-0482.** Pinata-making is an exciting children's activity offered at this center in the heart of the area's Hispanic population. Kids make their own pinatas, starting with an inflated balloon, then adding layers of paper, flour and water, and twine, then decorating it, and filling it with candy. *Time Frame:* 2-day sessions. *Ages:* 5 up. *Important to Know:* (I/R) (G/R) ($) (B) (D)

Kansas City, Kansas, Parks and Recreation Community Centers, 75 S. 23rd St., Kansas City, KS 66102, 371-4166. Pre-school programs for 4-year-olds are offered as well as summer and after-school programs that include gymnastics, drill team, ballet, sports such as boxing, arts and crafts, and other activities. *Ages:* 6 up. *Important to Know:* (I/R) ($ varies) (B)

Kansas State School for the Visually Handicapped, 1100 State Ave., Kansas City, KS 66102, 281-3308. Children with normal eyesight get a chance to understand what it's like for those who are visually impaired. The school will make a presentation at the location of your choice. There is a slide show, and a braille demonstration, and the use of the white cane is discussed. A speaker explains the problems inherent in communication and daily living skills to kids who hopefully can gain insight and empathy from the experience. *Time Frame:* 1 hour. *Ages:* 6 up. *Important to Know:* (G/R) ($) (D)

Missouri River Queen, 1 Kaw Point, Kansas City, KS 66101, 842-0027, 1-800-373-0027. Children can learn about the river and its history by taking an educational cruise of the river provided by the Missouri River Queen riverboat. It's tailored for the age group aboard. Ask for the information packet and coloring book which can be delivered to home or school. *Time Frame:* 1 hour. *Ages:* 3 up. *Important to Know:* (I/R) (G/R) ($) (B) (D)

SPECIAL EVENTS CALENDAR

MARCH

Youth Arts Month, Kaw Valley Arts Council and U.S.D. 500, P.O. Box 123324, Kansas City, KS 66112, 371-0024. (See The Arts, this section.) Held in conjunction with local schools, this month-long program for kids increases their awareness and appreciation of art. The itinerary includes a "Youth Happening Day" where children take part in T-shirt decoration, along with other art projects. There's also an art contest for elementary age school children and works by students are displayed at the Kaw Valley Arts Council Gallery, 753 State Avenue during this time. *Ages:* K to high school. *Important to Know:* supplies are donated except for the T-shirt decoration.

MAY

Piper Prairie Days, Piper Community Education Assoc., 12036 Leavenworth Rd., Kansas City, KS 66109, 721-2088. This two-day family event is a benefit for community education. There's a carnival, games, music, entertainment, a tractor pull, softball tournament, magic shows, clowns and more for kids. *Important to Know:* (D)

Polski Day, St. Joseph/St. Benedict Church, 8th and Vernon, Kansas City, KS 66102, 573-5700, 371-1837. Held to commemorate the Polish Constitution (like our July 4th), the day begins with a parade, a Polka Mass at the church, traditional dancing in costume, bands, games, and handmade toys from Poland. *Important to Know:* (No $)

JUNE

Quindaro Junteenth, Concerned Citizens for Old Quindaro, Quindaro Park, 34th and Sewell, Kansas City, KS 66104, 281-1678. This event celebrates the Emancipation Proclamation issued June 19 and, in this case, the heritage of Quindaro which was a "stop" on the underground railroad during the Civil War. The celebration includes a parade, food, games, pony rides, and entertainment. *Important to Know:* (No $)

Rosedale Festival, Rosedale Development Assoc., 3930 Rainbow Blvd., Kansas City, KS 66103, 677-5097. This community festival is a real social gathering with entertainment, food, crafts, and a children's area complete with a petting zoo, story tellers, an art contest, clown cars, and an "Ugly Dog" contest with prizes for the canine cuties. *Important to Know:* (No $)

JULY

Indian Pow Wow, Kansas City Indian Club, Wyandotte County Fairground, 1405 N. 98th St., Kansas City, KS 66111, 761-6313. This is a traditional gathering of native Americans from the area and an opportunity for them to share their culture with others. Crafts, traders, Indian foods, dance contests and more should please the kids. *Important to Know:* (No $)

AUGUST

Wyandotte County Fair, Wyandotte County Fair Assoc., 1405 N. 98th St., Kansas City, KS 66111, 788-7898. This typical county fair showcases the crafts, handiwork and skills of Wyandotte County residents. For kids: a petting zoo, carnival rides, entertainment, magicians, stilt walkers, and more. *Important to Know:* (No $) (D)

SEPTEMBER

Autumn Gold Parade and Festival, Leavenworth Rd. Assn., Westgate Bank Bldg., 6000 Leavenworth Rd., Kansas City, KS 66104, 788-3988. This community-spirited festival is definitely kid-oriented with a parade, family olympics, clowns, balloons, kiddie games, a 5-K run, rides, music and free gifts. *Important to Know:* ($ for the runs) (D)

Central Avenue Parade, Central Avenue Betterment Assoc., 969 Lowell Ave., Kansas City, KS 66101, 371-4511. Clowns, floats, marching bands, crafts booths, karate demonstrations and more are part of this celebration. *Important to Know:* (No $)

Grinter Applefest, The Friends of Grinter, 1420 S. 78th St., Kansas City, KS 66111, 299-0373. This old-fashioned family affair features demonstrations such as apple peeling using an antique apple peeler, a petting zoo, children's games, live entertainment, Civil War re-enactments, clowns, apple goodies of every kind, authentic 1800's curios, and crafts. *Important to Know:* (No $) (B)

OCTOBER

Silver City Day, Argentine Activity Assoc. and Argentine Optimists, 3218 Strong Ave., Kansas City, KS 66106, 831-2345. This event held right before the American Royal features a parade, arts and crafts and a children's area. *Important to Know:* (No $) (D)

Turner Days, Turner Board of Education and Turner Recreation Department, 1312 S. 55th St., Kansas City, KS 66106, 287-4000. This event, held to celebrate the progress of the Turner area, has a parade, entertainment provided primarily by children, a kiddie tractor pull, kid games, food, sky divers and more. *Important to Know:* (No $) (B) (D)

FUN EATS

Fritz's Union Station Restaurant, 250 N. 18th St. at Grandview Blvd., Kansas City, KS 66102, 281-2777. Kids can order their burgers and shakes by way of table telephone and watch in delight as their food is delivered by way of a model train system that runs about the tables. No train deliveries before 11 a.m. Waitresses deliver all drinks.

Marie's, 901 Kansas Ave., Kansas City, KS 66105, 281-2164. Aside from ice cream and the "Wizard" machine, kids like

Marie's homemade Italian sausage, meatball, steak and tenderloin sandwiches. The place specializes in great onion rings, too, and there are free balloons for tots.

McDonald's, 4101 Kansas Ave., Kansas City, KS 66106, 281-1312. Situated adjacent to the largest railroad yard in the country, this McDonald's has a real caboose that can be reserved for birthday parties. There's even a small train inside the caboose where children may sit. Group reservations only.

BONNER SPRINGS AND EDWARDSVILLE

HISTORIC SITES AND MUSEUMS

Agricultural Hall of Fame, 630 N. 126th St., Bonner Springs, KS 66012, 913-721-0175. The Ag Hall contains turn-of-the-century home and farm implements, a century-old railroad depot, blacksmith shop, a one-room schoolhouse, a nature trail and more. *Time Frame:* about 2 hours. *Ages:* 3rd to 6th grade (except tours). *Important to Know:* (I) (G/R) ($—kids under 5 are free) (B) (D)

Wyandotte County Museum, 631 N. 126th St., Wyandotte County Bonner Springs Park, Bonner Springs, KS 66012, 721-1078. The museum tells the history of Wyandotte County through exhibits that detail studies of pioneers like Lewis and Clark, the Wyandot Indians and early settlers. *Time Frame:* 45 minutes. *Ages:* pre-school up. *Important to Know:* (I) (G/R) (No $) (B) (D)

THE GREAT OUTDOORS

Special Area Parks and Playgrounds

Wyandotte County Bonner Springs Park, 126th and State Ave., Bonner Springs, KS 66012, 299-0550. This 640-acre park, site of Sandstone Amphitheater and the Renaissance Festival, is adjacent to the Agricultural Hall of Fame, and features ballfields, tennis courts, shelter houses, radio-controlled airplane flying field (permit required) and more. *Ages:* all. *Important to Know:* (I) (G) (No $) (B)

Special Programs and Exhibits

Nature Trail, Agricultural Hall of Fame, 630 N. 126th St., Bonner Springs, KS 66012, 913-721-1075. (Also see Historic Sites and Museums.) This mile-long trail on the museum premises has its specimens marked and identified. Tour guides are available. *Time Frame:* 30-45 minutes. *Ages:* all. *Important to Know:* (I) (G/R) ($) (B)

ENTERTAINING PEOPLE

Ann Miller, Naturalist, 10113 Steel Rd., Edwardsville, KS 66113, 913-422-5337. Miller's wildlife programs offer educational information on the importance of animals in our environment. She uses live animals in her demonstrations that include non-poisonous shakes and different mammals such as ferrets. Kids can touch the animals and ask questions. *Time Frame:* about 1 hour. *Ages:* all. *Important to Know:* (G/R) ($)

Pokey Dot the Clown, Ann Miller, 10113 Steel Rd., Edwardsville, KS 66113, 913-422-5337. Aside from her wildlife programs (see above) Ann Miller also specializes in party entertainment as Pokey Dot the Clown. Magic, games, crafts, face painting, and balloon animals are part of her show. *Time Frame:* about 1 hour. *Ages:* pre-school up. *Important to Know:* (G/R) ($)

SPECIAL EVENTS CALENDAR

AUGUST

Edwardsville Family Fun Days, City Recreation Commission, City Hall, 690 S. 4th St., P.O. Box 13243, Edwardsville, KS 66113, 913-441-3707. A parade kicks off Edwardsville's celebration of being the biggest small town in Wyandotte Co. There are booths, entertainment, tricycle races, games, clowns and more for kids. *Important to Know:* (No $)

Tiblow Days, Bonner Springs—Edwardsville Chamber of Commerce, P.O. Box 403, Bonner Springs, KS 66012, 913-441-4538. This event commemorates the founding of Bonner Springs by Henry Tiblow. Children like the parade, crafts fair, food, carnival, moonwalk, talent show and other entertainment. *Important to Know:* (No $)

SEPTEMBER AND OCTOBER

Renaissance Festival, Agricultural Hall of Fame grounds, 630 N. 126th St., Bonner Springs, KS 66011, 561-8005. The event which covers eight weekends is an authentic recreation of a 16th-century European village in the midst of a harvest celebration. There are jugglers, jesters, jousters, peasants, pirates, minstrels, puppets, games, magicians, mazes and children's shows, not to mention plenty of food. *Important to Know:* ($) (B) (D)

EASTERN JACKSON AND CASS COUNTIES, MISSOURI

FAIRMOUNT, SUGAR CREEK, INDEPENDENCE, BLUE SPRINGS, RAYTOWN, GRANDVIEW, LEE'S SUMMIT, AND BELTON-RAYMORE

KEY: (I) Individual tours, no reservations needed; (I/R) Individual tours by reservation; (G) group tours, no reservations needed; (G/R) group tours by reservation; (B) bathrooms; ($) fee; (No $) no fee; (D) some accommodations for the disabled.

FAIRMOUNT, SUGAR CREEK, INDEPENDENCE AND BLUE SPRINGS

ASSISTANCE

(NOTE: Missouri phone numbers have an 816 area code.)

Convention Bureaus and Chambers of Commerce

City of Independence, Division of Tourism, 111 E. Maple, Independence, MO 64050, 836-7111.

Independence Chamber of Commerce, 213 S. Main, Independence, MO 64051, 252-4745.

Blue Springs Chamber of Commerce, 202 S. 10th St., Blue Springs, MO 64015, 229-8558.

Clubs and Organizations

Kansas City, Missouri Council of Camp Fire. (See Assistance, East of Plaza, Kansas City, MO.)

Heart of America Council, Boy Scouts of America. (See Assistance, Kansas City, KS.)

Mid-Continent Council of Girl Scouts. (See Assistance, East of Plaza.)

YMCA of Greater Kansas City. (See Clubs and Organizations, Midtown.)

Special Assistance for the Disabled

Community Area Wide Transportation System, Inc., 8600 Old 23rd St., Kansas City, MO 64129, 461-3654. This organization provides door-to-door bus service for the disabled in the Greater Kansas City area.

Direction Service Center, 1511 Kingshighway, Independence, MO 64055, 833-4415. The center publishes a pamphlet featuring summer programs for disabled children. Abbreviated codes are used to determine handicapped conditions (LD, for Learning Disabled, BI, for Blind, etc.). Programs include day and residential camps and recreational and summer treatment programs. There are also private summer schools and public schools, plus camps and recreational programs not specifically designed for disabled.

The Whole Person, Inc., (See Special Assistance for the Disabled, South of Plaza, Kansas City, MO.) This is a private not-for-profit organization for people with disabilities.

Transportation

City Area Transportation Authority, 221-0660. The City subsidizes round-trip bus service from Blue Springs to Kansas City Monday through Friday.

Parks and Recreation Departments

Blue Springs Parks and Recreation, 903 Main, Blue Springs, MO 64015, 228-0137.

Jackson County Parks and Recreation, 22807 Woods Chapel Rd., Blue Springs, MO 64015, 795-8200.

Independence Parks and Recreation, 416 Maple, Independence, MO 64050, 836-7191.

BUSINESS AND COMMERCIAL TOURS

Blue Springs Bank, 1100 Main St., Blue Springs, MO 64015, 229-1111. This independent community bank was the first in the nation to establish a *children's* bank eight years ago. It is one of only three in the country. Tours include all departments and a visit to the vault. The bank also sponsors children's parties four times a year. Gifts await at the end of the tour. *Time Frame:* 35 minutes. *Ages:* pre-school up. *Important to Know:* (I/R) (G/R) (No $) (B) (D-limited)

Central Jackson County Fire Protection, Luttrell Rd. and U.S. 40, Blue Springs, MO 64015, 229-2522. This popular tour includes a look at the offices. The presentation gives youngsters a chance to observe how firemen work under pressure. Included is a visit with the "fire monster" (a fireman in a bunker suit), a look at equipment such as lights and sirens and how they work, and a discussion of fire safety. *Time Frame:* 30 minutes. Ages: pre-school up. *Important to Know:* (I/R) (G/R) (No $) (B) (D—limited)

Fairmont Dairy, 3805 Van Brunt Blvd., Extension, Kansas City, MO 64128, 921-7370. The tour covers everything from the milk delivery to actual bottle-making and processing of dairy products. Children get free milk or chocolate milk, and a special dairy treat as gifts. *Time Frame:* 30 minutes. *Ages:* 4 up. *Important to Know:* (I/R) (G/R) (No $) (B)

The Independence Examiner, 410 S. Liberty, Independence, MO 64050, 254-8600, Ext. 129. This Examiner serves Independence and Blue Springs, producing daily papers for these areas. The tour explains the operation and children get to see the reporters at work, how ads are designed, and how the presses run. *Time Frame:* 45 minutes. *Ages:* 3rd grade up. *Important to Know:* (G/R) (No $) (B) (D)

Independence Police Department (Officer Friendly), 223 N. Memorial Drive, Independence, MO 64050, 836-7208. Kids get to see the detective bureau, radio and squad rooms and, if possible, tour the jail. They'll learn about the law and how to keep it, plus they'll get plenty of safety tips. *Time Frame:* 30-45 minutes. *Ages:* 5 up. *Important to Know:* (I/R) (G/R) (No $) (B) (D)

RLDS Auditorium, 1001 West Walnut, Independence, MO 64050, 833-1000. This is the headquarters for the Reorganized Church of Jesus Christ of Latter Day Saints. The building holds a chamber which seats about 6,000 people and boasts a 110-rank Aeolian-Skinner organ, one of the largest church organs in the country. During the summer there are free organ recitals. *Time Frame:* between 15 minutes to an hour depending on whether an organ recital is given. *Ages:* all. *Important to Know:* (I) (G/R) (B) (No $) (D)

Shrout Brothers Dairy, Inc., U.S. 24 East, RR 2, Box 982, Independence, MO 64050, 796-2973. This is a working farm, with 300 head of cattle, complete with all the smells. City-bred kids, many of whom have never seen a cow being milked (let alone a cow) learn that milk doesn't really come from grocery store cartons. The tour includes watching milking operations and seeing baby calves. An explanation is given of how the milk is taken from the cows to the processing plants. *Time Frame:* 15 minutes. *Ages:* 1st grade up. *Important to Know:* (I) (G/R) (No $) (B—outdoors)

HISTORIC SITES AND MUSEUMS

Jackson County Parks and Recreation Heritage
Programs and Museums, Independence Square Courthouse, Room 205, Independence, MO 64050, 881-4431. This organization operates the many programs, events and historic sites in the area. They also publish a very informative newsletter and calendar of events which should be of great interest to families with children.

Harry S. Truman Library, 1200 N. McCoy, (U.S. 24 and Delaware St.), Independence, MO 64050, 833-1400. This presidential library contains exhibits on the Truman Presidency and related subjects. Of special children's interest is a brass replica of the USS Missouri which is over 18 feet long. Also on exhibit are the President's personal cars, including a 1941 Chrysler and a 1950 White House limousine. There is a reproduction of the oval office and table where the U.N. Charter was signed. The courtyard contains flags of the nation's states. *Time Frame:* 1 hour, depending on interest. *Ages:* all. *Important to Know:* (I) (G/R) (No $ for children under age 15) (B) (D)

Harry S. Truman Railroad Station, Grand and Pacific, Independence, MO 64050, 836-7111. This depot, which figured in Truman's 1948 "Whistle Stop" campaign, is listed on the National Register of Historic Places. There are historic exhibits in the station lobby where you can wait for daily Amtrak service into Kansas City. Round trip group rates are available and kids love the train ride. *Important to Know:* Amtrak service: (I/R) (G/R) ($) (B) (D)

Truman Home, 219 N. Delaware, Independence, MO 64050, 254-7199. Located in the Harry S. Truman National Landmark District, this was the home of President Harry S Truman and his wife, Bess Wallace Truman, until their deaths. Informative tours are conducted by park rangers who make it interesting for kids. *Time Frame:* the package includes a 12-minute slide show at the ticket center, a free shuttle bus to the Truman home and other historic sites, and a 30-minute tour of the residence. *Ages:* 1st grade up. *Important to Know:* individuals must reserve their tickets in person on a first-come, first-served basis at the Truman Home Ticket and Information Center, 223 N. Main St., 254-9929. (I/R) (G/R) ($) (B—inside Ticket and Information Center only)

Harry S. Truman Courtroom and Office, Independence Square Courthouse, Room 109, Main at Maple St., Independence, MO 64050, 881-4431. This is where the 33rd President of the United States began the political career that led him to the White House. You'll see Judge Truman's restored old quarters and an audio/visual presentation about Truman's life and courtship with Bess. *Time Frame:* the slide show is 30 minutes; the entire tour lasts 40-45 minutes. *Ages:* 2nd grade up. *Important to Know:* (I) (G/R) ($) (B) (D)

Harry S. Truman Historic District Walking Tour, between the HST Library and HST Home, Independence, MO 64050, 836-7111. Follow the route taken by Mr. Truman on one of his morning neighborhood walks. The mile-long self-guided tour takes you past a captivating assortment of architectural styles representing every decade since the 1860's. Children get lots of exercise and so will parents who can point out things of interest along the way. *Time Frame:* less than an hour. *Ages:* all, but bring strollers for tots. *Important to Know:* a self-guided tour brochure is available from the Independence Dept. of Tourism. (No $) (No B)

Bingham-Waggoner Estate, 313 W. Pacific, Independence, MO 64050, 461-3491. Built in 1855, this private home eventually became the residence of Missouri artist George Caleb Bingham who lived here with his wife, Eliza, until 1870. In 1879 the home was purchased by Peter and William Waggoner who remodeled the original structure which served as the family home until 1976. The 26-room residence is open to tour. Things of interest to children include over $5,000 worth of old toys and a stable and smokehouse. The root cellar is not usually open to the public, but the staff takes school age groups down to see it. *Time Frame:* 45 minutes to an hour. *Ages:* all. *Important to Know:* (I) (G/R) ($) (B—emergency only)

Brady Cabin and Spring, Noland and Truman Rds., Independence, MO 64050, 836-7111. This pioneer cabin, located near the site of an old spring, was built around 1830. It is furnished with an old feather bed, a cradle and spinning wheel, muzzle gun and other period items plus squirrel skins and an empty hornet's nest. Although this tour is self-guided, there are often volunteers on hand who explain the pioneer way of life to small children. The trip makes an interesting pit stop if you're in the area. *Time Frame:* about 10 minutes. *Ages:* pre-school up. *Important to Know:* Call in advance to find out if a volunteer will be in when you plan to visit. (I) (G) (No $) (No B) (D)

Dillingham-Lewis Home, 15th and Main, Blue Springs, MO 64015, 229-1671. This early 20th-century pioneer home holds tours and offers several special events during the year. Kids are fascinated by the old furnace vents, ice cream freezer, Victrola, pump, vacuum cleaner and other old artifacts on the premises. *Time Frame:* about 40 minutes. *Ages:* 7 up. *Important to Know:* (I) (G/R) (No $) (B)

Fort Osage, Sibley, Mo., 14 miles northeast of Independence. U.S. 24 east to Buckner. Turn north at Sibley St. and follow the signs. 881-4431. Built in 1808 by William Clark of Lewis and Clark fame, this first U.S. outpost in the Louisiana Purchase has lots of frontier buildings for children to explore, as well as Osage Indian artifacts and exhibits reflecting the area's early history. (Also see Special Activities.) *Time Frame:* anywhere from 45 minutes up. *Ages:* 2nd grade up. *Important to Know:* lots of walking, so bring sturdy shoes. (I) (G/R) ($) (B)

Vaile Mansion-DeWitt Museum, 1500 N. Liberty St., Independence, MO 64050, 833-0040. One of the best examples of Victorian architecture in the U.S., the 1882 mansion's second floor has a smoking room with woodwork painted with dozens of little faces and animals. Children find it intriguing to search for them. Also of note is a mini post office. *Time Frame:* about 40 minutes. *Ages:* 2nd grade up. *Important to Know:* tell children not to touch anything from furniture to walls. (I) (G) ($) (B)

1859 Marshall's Home & Jail Museum, 217 N. Main St., Independence, MO 64050, 252-1892. Four buildings comprise this museum including the jail which held Frank James, the marshall's restored home, a one-room school-house and a county museum. Children seem to be very interested in the jail cells, especially when they learn the youngest prisoner here was only nine years old! The school-house accommodates four children and was heated by a wood-burning stove. *Time Frame:* 1 hour. *Ages:* 4th grade up. *Important to Know:* (I) (G/R) ($) (No B)

Missouri Town 1855, Fleming Park, Blue Springs, MO. Head east on I-70, south on M-291. Take a left at Colbern Road exit to Cyclone School Road. Go left and follow signs. 881-4431. This reconstructed 1850s farming community is comprised of over 30 original structures that make up a charming village. Children love the opportunity to see barnyard animals such as free-running chickens, plus sheep and horses. The volunteer staff, dressed in period attire, loves to kibbitz with the kids while demonstrating chores done by frontier Americans. *Time Frame:* 45 minutes but families can set their own pace. *Ages:* 1st grade up. *Important to Know:* (I) (G/R) ($) (B)

THE ARTS

The Kindermusik Playce, 1316 N. Kiger, Independence, MO 64040, 254-5853. Developed in West Germany, this program affords children a positive musical experience by helping them discover their abilities and interest in music through a variety of games and dramatization. Instruction in voice training, musical notation and note values, ensemble experience, improvisation and creativity are stressed in this two-year course. Kids get a special bag to carry materials to class, plus a colorful music folder, stickers, badges, and a portable *glockenspiel* for home practice. *Time Frame:* hour class sessions. *Ages;* 4 to 6. *Important to Know:* (I/R) ($) (B)

AMUSEMENTS

Bally's Alladin's Castle, 1026 Independence Center, in the Mall, Independence, MO 64057, 795-0225. A clean, well-maintained family fun center located in a shopping mall and adult-supervised. *Ages:* 8 up. *Important to Know:* birthday parties are held here. ($) (B) (D)

Cool Crest Garden Golf, 10713-10735 E. 40 Hwy., (1/2 Mile W. of Blue Ridge Mall), Independence, MO 64055, 358-0088. Miniature golf, plus a game room which offers pinball and video machines, snooker and pocket billiards provides clean, wholesome fun. *Ages:* 8 up. *Important to Know:* ($) (B)

40-Hi Batting Range, 10789E. U.S. 40, Independence, MO 64055, 356-8088. A batting range provides baseball and slow pitch softball. There's a go-cart track with a height requirement. Helmets are provided. A small arcade is on the premises. *Ages:* 9 up. *Important to Know:* ($) (B)

Jacomo Waterslide, in Lake Jacomo by the swimming beach, mailing address is P.O. Box 88, Lee's Summit, MO 64063, 524-9875. The privately-owned waterslides are over 4,500 feet long and empty into a pool here to provide summer excitement for kids. *Ages:* 1st grade up. *Important to Know:* concessions ($) (B)

Kansas City International Raceway, 8201 Noland Rd., Kansas City, MO 64138, 358-6700. Drag racing, street stocks, high performance and funny cars provide the entertainment here. Kids often come along, making this a family outing for racing enthusiasts. *Ages:* all. Smaller children may be bothered by the loud noise. *Important to Know:* concessions available. ($) (B)

Space Port, 4200 Blue Ridge Blvd., Blue Ridge Mall, Kansas City, MO 64133, 353-5225. This arcade has plenty of games and is supervised by attendants. *Ages:* 8 up. *Important to Know:* ($) (B in mall located near the arcade) (D)

White Oak Fun Center, 1007 S. M-7, Blue Springs, MO 64015, 229-6440. This center offers a "snack shop," plus video games. *Ages:* 8 up. *Important to Know:* ($) (B) (D)

SPORTS

B and D Rolladium-South, 36th and Noland Ct., Independence, MO 64055, 252-1084. Open to the public, the rink is also available for private parties and features organized family nights. *Important to Know:* ($) (B)

Blue Springs Rolladium Skating Rink, 513 Keystone Dr., Blue Springs, MO 64015, 229-7793. The rink has organized family nights suitable to all schedules. It's also available for private parties. *Important to Know:* ($) (B)

Centennial Pool-Plex, 2401 Ashton Drive, Blue Springs, MO 64015, 228-0188, 228-0137. This public swimming facility includes 25-yard, 50-meter, and kiddie pools. A major advantage: the 82-degree, 25-yard pool is open in winter when the place isn't so crowded. *Ages:* all. *Important to Know:* showers and concessions are available. ($) (B) (D)

Great American Gymnastics Express, 1001 W. Jefferson, Blue Springs, MO 64015, 229-7775. Children participate in a variety of gymnastics that provide a strong physical fitness program' for kids. *Ages:* 1½ and over. *Important to Know:* (I/R) ($) (B) (D)

Pool Party, Fleming Park at Lake Jacomo, 22807 Woods Chapel Rd., Blue Springs, MO 64015, 795-8556. Plan a pool party for groups of 50 or less in summer at Kemper Gardens, home of Jacomo Day Camp. Reservations include the use of the shelterhouse, grills, games, playground and more. *Ages:* all. *Important to Know:* available weekends and holidays. Rental application needed. There is no electricity, telephone, or fishing at the pond. ($) (B)

Sterling Bowl, 11216 E. U.S. 24, Sugar Creek, MO 64052, 252-2111. There's a bowling league and lessons for kids. *Ages:* all. *Important to Know:* (I) (G/R) ($) (B) (D)

Sugar Creek Pool, Kentucky and Sterling Rds., Sugar Creek, MO 64054, 254-7645. This neighborhood jewel is the site for parties, swim competitions and swim lessons for kids. There are life guards and special areas for tots. *Ages:* all. *Important to Know:* (I) (G) ($) (B)

PLAYING TOGETHER

Instructional League, 104 S. Hedges, Sugar Creek, MO 64054, 252-3242. This league is for kids who want to play baseball but haven't learned how. They're taught the basics and play other teams with the same training, often gaining needed self-confidence. The parents can coach, umpire or referee. *Ages:* 8 to 10. *Important to Know:* (I/R) (No $) (B) (D)

Kid/Adult Fitness Class, Sermon Center, 201 Dodgion, Independence, MO 64050, 836-7195. These fitness classes offer parent-child interaction in games, sing songs and exercise activities. The sessions strive to strengthen the child's emotional well-being and development. *Ages:* infants up. *Important to Know:* (I/R) ($) (B)

THE GREAT OUTDOORS

Special Programs and Exhibits

Kid's Fishing Derby, Lake Jacomo Shelter House #6, #7, 22807 Woods Chapel Rd., Blue Springs, MO 64015, 795-8556. This annual May event brings kids from around the city to compete for prizes. Fishing gear donated by local merchants is awarded to the winners. *Ages:* 2 to 15. *Important to Know:* fishing license not required. All children must be accompanied by an adult. (No $) (B)

Moonlight Pontoon Tours of Lake Jacomo, Fleming Park, 22807 Woods Chapel Rd., Blue Springs, MO 64015, 795-8556. Join interpretive Park Rangers for a moonlight pontoon boat tour of the lake. It's casual, so dress warmly; bring binoculars and refreshments for the boat ride. *Time Frame:* 2 hours. *Ages:* all. The ride may be too long for some youngsters. *Important to Know:* kids must be accompanied by an adult. ($) (B—available at the marina and park)

Special Area Parks and Playgrounds

Most area parks offer picnic areas, ball fields, tennis courts, playgrounds, shelters and more. Phone the Independence or Blue Springs Parks and Recreation Depts. (See Assistance, this section.) In the meantime, this is a sampling of what you'll find:

Dickinson Pool and Park, 1700 Dickinson Rd., Independence, MO. A pool with concessions is open during summer.

Fleming Park, M-291 and Woods Chapel Rd., Blue Springs, MO. There are 7,000 acres available for public recreation. Included are facilities for boating, archery, camping, fishing, hiking, and Missouri Town. Migrating waterfowl also visit the area in winter.

Pink Hill Park, N. M-7 and Park Road, Blue Springs, MO. Has a BMX race track and is adjacent to Burr Oak Woods. (D)

Railroad Lake Park, S. M-7 and Vesper St., Blue Springs, **MO.** Has walking trails, a fishing lake, and equipment centering around a railroad theme. A 22-foot gazebo is available by reservation. Free concerts are held there in August on Sunday nights, so bring a lawn chair or blankets.

Nature Sanctuaries

Burr Oak Woods Nature Center, 1401 Park Road (N. M-7 and Park Road), Blue Springs, MO 64015, 228-3766. Over 1,000 acres of exhibits, wildlife habitat and discovery trails and picnic areas comprise this urban forest and wildlife refuge. Children love exhibits that feature deer, snakes, frogs, ducks and a bald eagle, plus a fish aquarium stocked with native fish. There is also an outdoor bird feeding area where youngsters can view the creatures in their environment. Special nature hikes, and classes are available. *Time Frame:* 30 minutes to all day. *Ages:* all. *Important to Know:* A city park adjacent to the center offers a 40-acre playground area. There's a drinking fountain inside the center. (I) (G/R) (No $) (B) (D)

George Owens Nature Park, 1601 S. Speck Rd., Independence, MO 64057, 257-4654. The park has two fishing lakes, walking trails, and a nature center with an outdoor habitat filled with live deer, bats, geese and snakes. Films are offered on Saturdays once a month. *Time Frame:* 30 minutes to 2 hours. *Ages:* all. *Important to Know:* (G/R for shelter house) ($ for shelter house) (B)

Outdoor Education Programs

Burrough's Audubon Center and Library, off Woods Chapel Rd., near the marina of Lake Jacomo, Blue Springs, MO 64105, 795-8177. Children learn about nature at the center which contains exhibits of birds nests, insects and butterflies. Outdoor bird feeders bring in a variety of birds to watch each day. Tours of the place include a slide show. *Time Frame:* 30 minutes. *Ages:* all. *Important to Know:* (I) (G/R) (No $) (B)

Nature Hikes and Campfire Programs and Interpretive Programs, Fleming Park at Lake Jacomo, 22807 Woods Chapel Rd., Blue Springs, MO 64015, 795-8556. Kids can join park rangers on an interpretive nature hike or for a program around a blazing campfire. Waterfowl and mushroom hikes, stargazing and mythology, live snake presentations and fishing clinics are part of the fun. Parents can go along, if they wish. *Ages:* all. *Important to Know:* programs are scheduled for spring, summer and fall. (I) (G/R) ($) (B)

Outdoor Recreation Trips, Jackson County Parks and Recreation, Fleming Park at Lake Jacomo, 22807 Woods Chapel Rd., Blue Springs, MO 64105, 795-8556.2 The three-day float trips offered include transportation, meals, canoes, camping fees, paddles, lifejackets and staff and run from spring through fall. Some waterways include the Current, North Fork and Meramec Rivers. Trips can include horseback riding, camping and fishing. *Ages:* 10 up. Must be accompanied by parent. *Important to Know:* ($)

Summer Camping Programs

Jacomo Day Camp, Kemper Gardens, Fleming Park at Lake Jacomo, 22807 Woods Chapel Rd., Blue Springs, MO 64015, 795-8556. Exciting supervised outdoor activities here include swimming, archery, fishing, hiking, sailing, nature study, arts and crafts, sports and games and more. Overnight campouts are optional. Five sessions are offered, each lasting two weeks. Day campers bring their own sack lunch and a beverage is provided. *Time Frame:* all day. *Ages:* 6-12. *Important to Know:* "Extended Hours Service" provides supervision for kids who get there early and stay late. ($)

YMCA of Greater Kansas City, 3100 Broadway, Suite 930, Kansas City, MO 64111, 561-9622. The YMCA has an abundance of sports and cultural programs for kids, plus day camps, child care, and other offerings. Rather than trying to list them all in our limited space, we suggest calling the main number for information on the YMCA location nearest you.

SPECIAL LIBRARY PROGRAMS

Mid-Continent Public Libraries. *The Mid-Continent Library system has a summer reading program. Children can receive a free paperback for every 20 books they read. The library also offers movies and puppet shows. Ages: preschool to primary school. Important to Know: library cards are available to children as soon as they can sign their names, otherwise parents can check the books out. (D)*

Blue Springs Branch, 2220 S. M-7, Blue Springs, MO 64015, 229-3571.

North Independence Branch, Spring St. and W. U.S. 24, Independence, MO 64050, 252-0950.

South Independence Branch, 13901 Noland Ct., Independence, MO 64055, 461-2050.

Harry S. Truman Library, U.S. 24 and Delaware St., Independence, MO 64050, 833-1400. (See Historic Sites and Museums.)

ENTERTAINING PEOPLE

Ace High Entertainers and Klamm, 1412 Appleton, Independence, MO 64052, 461-4595. This organization features Klamm the Magic Man and other magicians and clowns to entertain at parties, special events and school and organization functions. Children get to participate in the fun. Book ahead. *Important to Know:* ($)

Candy and Momo's Family Circus, phone only, 254-3184. Candy is the magician; Momo, the ventriloquist. Together they provide parties for children's birthdays, entertaining together as clowns, elves, or bunnies. Their acts include magic shows, balloon animals, face painting, trained birds, pony rides, and more. There's plenty of audience participation as kids interact during the shows and sing-alongs. *Time Frame:* 30-45 minutes. Ages: 1 year up. *Important to Know:* (G/R) ($)

SPECIAL ACTIVITIES

Harry S. Truman Railroad Station, Grand and Pacific, Independence, MO 64050, 836-7111. (See Historic Sites and Museums, this section.)

Independence Farmer's Market, Truman Rd. between Osage St. and White Oak Ave., Independence, MO 64050, 373-8347. Farmers from around the area come to sell their produce here on Saturdays from May to September. Children used to seeing plastic-wrapped produce get a chance to taste fresh-from-the-ground veggies. It's a good education and a different kind of adventure. *Ages:* all. *Important to Know:* (No B)

Osage Honey Farm, Sibley, MO, 14 miles northeast of Independence. U.S. 24 east to Buckner, a few blocks south of Fort Osage, 816-249-5637. Missouri honey is offered for sale here. Children enjoy watching bees at work in the glass-enclosed hive on the premises. Bus tours of children can be taken through the honey operation with advance notice. *Ages:* all. *Important to Know:* (B)

Apple Spot Orchard, Sibley, MO, 14 miles northeast of Independence. U.S. 24 east to Buckner, a few blocks south of Fort Osage, 816-249-5363. Children love picking their own fruit for apple pie fixings from this orchard which is right down the road from the Osage Honey Farm. You can bring your own bushel basket, or borrow one from the Apple Spot. *Important to Know:* ($) (No B)

Sermon Center, 201 Dodgion (Noland and Truman Rds.), Independence, MO 64050, 836-7195. (Also see Playing Together, this section.) The center has weight and game rooms for kids, plus volleyball, gymnastics, parent-child fitness classes, craft classes and much more. The Center's theater presents a children's show each year. *Ages:* all. *Important to Know:* (I/R) ($) (B)

Stephenson's Orchard, 6700 Lee's Summit Rd., Kansas City, MO 64136, 373-5138. Close enough to Independence to justify inclusion in this section, Stephenson's is the place to bring the kids during apple or strawberry-picking time. Just watch the newspaper to see when the orchard is open to the public. Your little taste-tester is going to love picking fruit from branches so low to the ground even a two-year-old can reach the apples. Once it's picked, it's back home to bake the pie. *Ages:* all. *Important to Know:* there is some walking. (about 1/4 mile) involved to reach the strawberry fields. Apple orchards are easily accessed by car. ($) (No B)

Shuttle Bus, Independence Division of Tourism, Truman Ticket Information Center, Main St. at Truman Rd., 836-7111. Independence provides a free shuttle operating daily at 15-minute intervals to various historic sites. Tours begin at the Truman Ticket Information Center and proceed from there to the Truman Home, Bingham-Waggoner Estate, Truman Library and Museum, Vaile Mansion and other attractions. *Important to Know:* (No $)

SPECIAL EVENTS CALENDAR

APRIL

Spring Rendezvous, Independence Square, Chamber of Commerce, Independence Square, Independence, MO 64050, 252-4745. Spinning, weaving and other old-time crafts are demonstrated. Fur traders, trappers and black-smiths are on hand to talk to kids. *Important to Know:* (No $)

MAY

Riverdays Celebration, Fort Osage, Sibley, MO, 14 miles northeast of Independence. U.S. 24 east to Buckner. Turn north at Sibley St. and follow the signs, 881-4431. The event is a celebration of river life as it was in the early 1800s and includes period camps, crafts, and skill competitions, plus food and entertainment. Trappers and traders are on hand to demonstrate fire starting and flintlock muskets. A special children's area promotes games played during the era. *Important to Know:* ($)

JUNE

Children's Day, Missouri Town 1855, East Side, Fleming Park at Lake Jacomo, Blue Springs, MO 64015, 881-4431. Bring your child here to experience what life was like back in 1855. Children's games, contests, stories, chores, spinning and weaving, and more await. The hands-on experience of candle-dipping and lemonade-squeezing add to the fun. Period games include hoop rolling and jacks. *Important to Know:* (No $ for children 13 and under when accompanied by an adult)

Slavic Festival, Mike Onca Building, Sugar Creek, MO 64054, 252-4400. The rich Slavic heritage of the area is celebrated when Sugar Creek hosts this event that boasts dancing, entertainment and food such as cabbage rolls and *Povatica*. There are souvenirs, Slavic games and dancing for the kids. *Important to Know:* ($)

Vaile Fancy Faire and Strawberry Festival, Vaile Victorian Society, Vaile Mansion Dewitt Museum, 1500 N. Liberty, Independence, MO 64050, 833-0040. Homes tours, strawberry ice cream contest, puppet show, and buggy rides top off the entertainment at this event held on the grounds of the Vaile Mansion. A flea market and craft show gets adult attention, while a children's corner for ages 5 to 12 holds activities to acquaint youngsters with the Victorian era. *Important to Know:* ($ for house tour)

JULY

Independence Day at Missouri Town 1855, Fleming Park at Lake Jacomo, Blue Springs, MO 64015, 881-4431. A day-long celebration of the most popular mid-19th-century holiday features traditional ceremonies, parades, a children's fair, a fish fry, watermelon and lemonade. This is a good daytime jaunt to take before the evening's activities. *Important to Know:* ($)

Independence Day at Fort Osage, U.S. 24 and BB Rd., Sibley, MO 64088, 881-4431. Friends of the Fort help celebrate in 1812 style. This is a good daytime event before starting the evening's activities. *Important to Know:* ($)

SEPTEMBER

Blue Springs Fall Fun Festival, 9th to 12th and Main in Blue Springs, MO 64015, 228-6322. This street festival features 300 arts and crafts booths, entertainment and refreshments. A special area for children provides games, carnival and pony rides, a petting zoo and a "pet parade." Lots of walking is involved so bring strollers for the young ones. Portable bathrooms on the premises. *Important to Know:* (No $) (D)

Fort Osage Open Rendezvous and Flint Knap-In, Fort Osage, U.S. 24 and BB Rd., Sibley, MO 64088, 881-4431. Trappers, traders and artisans gather to share their knowledge of a colorful historic era. The craftspeople shape primitive tools, knives and arrowheads from stone and are fascinating for kids to watch. *Important to Know:* ($)

Santa-Cali-Gon Days, Chamber of Commerce, Independence Square, Independence, MO 64050, 252-4745. This Labor Day weekend celebration commemorates the Santa Fe, California and Oregon trails that lead from Independence. Kids like the carnival atmosphere complete with games, food, booths, entertainment, and rides. *Important to Know:* ($ for rides) (D)

OCTOBER

Missouri Town 1855 Festival of Arts, Crafts, and Music, Fleming Park at Lake Jacomo, Blue Springs, MO 64105, 881-4431. Old-time arts, crafts, and music, plus dancing and demonstrations are part of the family fun. Friendly interpreters in period attire play 1850's-style games with the kids. Great apple cider, surrey rides, and good food make this event a must. *Important to Know:* ($)

DECEMBER

Christmas at Missouri Town, Fleming Park at Lake Jacomo, Blue Springs, MO 64015, 881-4431. This recreation of an 1850's Christmas party has activities that include storytelling, sing-alongs, caroling, demonstrations and food. There's a yule long on the fire to pop popcorn, and cookies are made over the open hearth. It's going to be cold, so bundle up the kids. *Important to Know:* (No $)

FUN EATS

(Also check multiple restaurant locations under Kansas City, MO.)

Show Biz Pizza Place, 4029 S. Noland Rd., Independence, MO 64055, 254-6300. This popular family place has pizza, hot dogs, a salad bar and stage show, plus a game room with kiddie rides, ski ball, and videos. Birthday packages require advance reservations.

Stephenson's Apple Farm Restaurant, U.S. 40 E. at Lee's Summit Rd., Kansas City, MO 64136, 373-5400. Close enough to Independence to be featured in this section, the family restaurant has kid-sized portions of its famous smoked chicken, ham and pork chops. Children love the luscious apple dumplings and free apple cider.

Fast Food Havens, on M-7 between I-70 south to U.S. 40, in Blue Springs, MO. If you're looking for a quick burger, chicken, pizza, barbecue, Chinese food, fish, tacos, deli or steaks you'll find it all within this mile strip that lines the "main drag" of town.

Fast Food Havens, Noland Rd., south of 23rd St., past I-70 and to U.S. 40, all located in a 3-4 mile area. Offerings range from seafood, barbecue and steaks to pizza, hamburgers, chicken and deli fare.

GOODIES

Swartz Old World Bakery, 3010 S. M-291, Independence, MO 64057, 478-0515. This establishment specializes in coconut macaroons and brownies. The made-from-scratch sweets also include eclairs, cream pies and cakes. *Important to Know:* (D)

Clinton's Old Fashioned Soda Fountain and Gift Shop, 100 W. Maple, Independence, MO 64050, 833-2625. This is where Harry S. Truman obtained his first job making $3 a week when he was 14. The store has been restored to its yesteryear look. Old timey treats include phosphates, fresh squeezed lemonade and limeade, plus sodas, floats, milkshakes, and banana splits served in glass containers.

RAYTOWN, GRANDVIEW, LEE'S SUMMIT

ASSISTANCE

Convention Bureaus and Chambers of Commerce

Raytown Chamber of Commerce, 11531 E. 63rd St., Raytown, MO 64133, 353-8500.

Grandview Chamber of Commerce, Grandview Bank Building, 12500 S. U.S. 71, Grandview, MO 64030, 761-6505.

Lee's Summit Chamber of Commerce, 610 S.E. M-291, Lee's Summit, MO 64063, 524-2424.

Clubs and Organizations

YMCA Of Greater Kansas City. (See Clubs and Organizations, Midtown, Kansas City, MO)

Special Assistance—Day Care

Child Care Connection, 442 S.W. Sunset Dr., Lee's Summit, MO 64081, 524-2287.

Special Assistance for the Disabled

HandiKab, Box 927, Lee's Summit, MO 64063, 525-2929. Serves the elderly or disabled in the metropolitan area and is wheelchair-equipped.

Transportation

Bannister Cab Co., 1523 Main St., Grandview, MO 64030, 444-3672.

Lee's Summit Limousine and Taxi Cab, P.O. Box 148, Blue Springs, MO 64015, 524-6333.

Parks and Recreation Departments

Grandview Parks and Recreation Department, 1200 Main, Grandview, MO 64030, 763-3900, Ext. 63.

Lee's Summit Parks and Recreation Department, 307 S. Market, Lee's Summit, MO 64063, 525-5777.

Raytown Parks and Recreation Department, 5912 Lane, Raytown, MO 64133, 358-4100.

HISTORIC SITES AND MUSEUMS

Raytown Museum, 9705 E. 63rd St., Raytown, MO 64133, 353-5033. Established by the Raytown Historical Society the museum is housed in a former fire station where exhibits date back to the early 1800's. There's a general store and blacksmith shop as well as other displays that include a classroom with old desks, books and lunch boxes. *Time Frame:* about 30 minutes. *Ages:* pre-school up. *Important to Know:* (I) (G/R) (No $) (B)

The Truman Farm Home, 12301 Blue Ridge Blvd., Grandview, MO 64030, 881-4431. This was President Harry S.
Truman's home from 1906 to 1917. Children are usually interested in the ceramic chamber pot, since they can't imagine a home without indoor plumbing. Because there are no closets, simple things like clothes hooks also get their attention. Since few kids know much about farm life, they might like learning about how young Truman did his chores. *Time Frame:* about 20 minutes. *Ages:* pre-school up. *Important to Know:* caution children not to touch furniture or walls. (I) (G/R) ($) (No B)

Unity School of Christianity (Unity Village), M-350 and Colbern Rd., Unity Village, MO 64065, 524-3550. Unity
Village is the headquarters of the Worldwide Unity Movement, a non-denominational religious educational organization. Visitors see a 20-minute slide presentation, and tour *Wee Wisdom* magazine publishing facility, the library, rose garden and activity center. *Time Frame:* 90-minute walking tour. *Ages:* 9 years up with an adult for every 10 children. *Important to Know:* (I) (G/R) (No $) (B) (D)

AMUSEMENTS

Hickman Mills Fun Center, 11320 Hickman Mills Dr., Kansas City, MO 64134, 763-4343. This facility has two
miniature golf courses, go-carts, bumper boats, game room and more. *Ages:* all. *Important to Know:* ($) (B)

Lee's Summit Railroad Station, 220 S. Main, Lee's Summit, MO 64063, no phone. Amtrak provides service from
Lee's Summit to Amtrak's downtown Kansas City station across from Crown Center. You and your child could hop aboard just for fun, and have someone pick you up on the other end, or take the return train back after exploring the

Crown Center area. *Time Frame:* the train takes less than an hour. *Ages:* all. *Important to Know:* call Amtrak before leaving for the station to find out if the train's on time. Tickets can be obtained at the downtown Kansas City office, from a travel agent, or aboard the train. Check for current times and rates. ($) (B)

SPORTS

Landmark Skate Center of Lee's Summit, U.S. 291 and U.S. 50, Lee's Summit, MO 64063, 524-2000. The rink is open to the public and offers organized family nights as well as private parties. *Important to Know:* ($) (B)

Raytown Public Pool, 53rd Place and Raytown Rd., Raytown, MO 64133, 356-5300 (pool); 358-4100. This public facility has a 50-meter and children's wading pool, concession area, volleyball courts, and a playground. Open in summer. *Important to Know:* ($ for pool) (B)

Skateland of Grandview, 13613 S. U.S. 71, Grandview, MO 64030, 763-3220. Open to the public, the rink has organized family nights in addition to private party bookings. *Important to Know:* ($) (B)

THE GREAT OUTDOORS

Special Area Parks and Playgrounds

Most area parks offer picnic areas, ball fields, tennis courts, playgrounds, shelters and more. Phone the Parks and Recreation Department in your area for more information. (See Assistance, this section.) In the meantime, this is a sampling of what you'll find:

John Anderson Park and Swim Pool, 4701 E. 135th St., Grandview, MO. A "showcase" park, the facility also includes a pool and amphitheater housed in a rustic wooded setting.

Coleman-Livengood Park, 59th and Lane, Raytown, MO.

Harris Park (Lee's Summit Municipal Pool), 605 S.W. Jefferson, Lee's Summit, MO. Has a public swimming pool with concessions.

Kenagy Park, 79th and Raytown Rd., Raytown, MO. Has a fishing pond.

Longview Lake, I-470 S. between Lee's Summit and Grandview, Lee's Summit, MO. Once a part of Longview Farm, this 4,762-acre park features a model airfield for radio control aircraft, bike paths, boating, fishing, swimming, hiking, and horseback riding. The swimming beach has a large area of shallow water where kids can splash.

Meadowmere Park and Swim Pool, 13610 Byars Rd., Grandview, MO. One of two "showcase" parks in Grandview, this facility also includes an olympic-size pool, heritage tree collection, pond and a pavilion.

Nature Sanctuaries

James A. Reed Memorial Wildlife Area, 13101 Ranson Rd., Lee's Summit, MO 64063, 524-1656. This Missouri

Conservation Department area has fishing lakes and nature trails that are abundant with song birds, deer, migrating waterfowl and other wildlife. There are fishing clinics for kids 12 and younger at the children's pond which is well-stocked for a guaranteed catch. *Ages:* all. *Important to Know:* Self-guided tours, rather than group tours are encouraged. ($ for fishing and hunting) (B in Visitor Center)

Summer Camping Programs

John Anderson Day Camp, 4701 E. 135th St., Grandview, MO 64030, 763-3900, Ext. 63. A qualified staff runs this day camp with one counselor for 10 children. Snacks, cookouts, swimming lessons, arts and crafts, and field trips are part of the activities. *Time Frame:* daily, Monday through Friday. *Ages:* 5 to 12 years. *Important to Know:* naps are given to younger children. ($)

Longview Day Camp, Longview Lake, I-470 S. between Lee's Summit and Grandview, Lee's Summit, MO 64063, 795-8556. Supervised outdoor education activities include swimming, archery, arts and crafts, horseback riding, overnight campouts and much more. Day campers bring a sack lunch, and a beverage is provided. The sessions last two weeks. *Ages:* 6 to 12. *Important to Know:* "Extended Hours Services" provides supervision for kids who arrive early and stay late. ($)

Meadowmere Day Camp, 13610 Byars Rd., Grandview, MO 64030, 763-3900, Ext. 63. Supervised activities include arts and crafts, swimming, cookouts and special field trips. *Ages:* 5 to 12. *Important to Know:* ($)

YMCA of Greater Kansas City, 3100 Broadway, Suite 930, Kansas City, MO 64111, 561-9622. The YMCA has an abundance of sports and cultural programs for kids, plus day camps, child care, and other offerings. Rather than trying to list them all in our limited space, we suggest calling the main number for information on the YMCA location nearest you.

SPECIAL LIBRARY PROGRAMS

Mid-Continent Public Library, Raytown Branch, 10016 E. 62nd St., Raytown, MO 64133, 353-2052. (See Special Library Programs, Blue Springs.)

Mid-Continent Public Library, Lee's Summit Branch, 901 W. O'Brien Rd., Lee's Summit, MO 64063, 524-0567. (See Special Library Programs, Blue Springs.)

Mid-Continent Public Library, Grandview Branch, 12930 Booth Lane, Grandview, MO 64030, 763-0550. (See Special Library Programs, Blue Springs.)

ENTERTAINING PEOPLE

Duane Field, 1137 Country Lane Place, Lee's Summit, MO 64063, 525-0021. Field entertains groups with his sophisticated magic act. Kids like the visuals: colorful props and plenty of fire and flash. *Ages:* all. *Important to Know:* ($) (D)

SPECIAL ACTIVITIES

Chapman Farm Orchard, Mason School Rd. and M-7, about 5 miles south of Blue Springs, Lee's Summit, MO 64063, 228-4924 (seasonal phone). Pick your own strawberries and corn in this orchard. Strawberry patches are close to the parking area and children are given their own individual boxes for collecting the juicy fruit. *Ages:* all. *Important to Know:* there's some walking involved, so equip the kids with good shoes and old clothes. ($) (B—outdoors)

Powell Horticultural and Natural Resources Center, Route #1, Box 90, Kingsville, MO 64061, (15 miles E. of Lee's Summit on U.S. 50), 816-566-2600. Year-around programs are given for school and youth groups and include over 30 horticultural and nature topics for kids. Children's sessions feature everything from Missouri snakes and birds to astronomy programs and wildflower walks. *Time Frame:* about 2 hours. Individuals are welcome to stroll the grounds and hike the nature trails at their leisure. *Ages:* pre-school through high school. *Important to Know:* (G/R for youth programs) ($) (B)

Richards-Gebaur Air Force Base Air Show, S. U.S. 71 in Grandview, Grandview, MO 64063, 348-2228, 348-2000. Held each summer, this is one of the country's largest airshows. The two-day event is highlighted by exciting air feats by Air Force jets, complete with smoke and sound. Exhibits of planes, concessions, movies, and rides round out the fare. *Important to Know:* (No $) (B)

SPECIAL EVENTS CALENDAR

MAY

Harry's Hay Days, Grandview Heritage Commission, Truman Corners Shopping Center, Blue Ridge and U.S. 71, Grandview, MO 64063, 763-3900, Ext. 63. Live entertainment, fun and games are held to celebrate the birth of President Harry S Truman, who lived on his Grandview farm from 1906-1917. Kids like the carnival atmosphere, complete with rides and a petting zoo. *Important to Know:* (No $)

JUNE

Cole Younger Days, Lee's Summit Chamber of Commerce, Chipman and N. Douglas Road, Lee's Summit, MO 64063, 524-2424. This old-fashioned family celebration carries a western theme courtesy of the outlaws who became folk heroes. Carnival games, booths, food and entertainment for everyone, plus arts and crafts for kids. *Important to Know:* (No $)

FUN EATS

Fun House Pizza & Pub, 9120 E. U.S. 350, Raytown, MO 64133, 356-5141. In addition to pizza, this restaurant keeps the kids busy with a merry-go-round, videos, television and rides. Children also can watch pizzas being made. (D)

Fast Food Havens, the 9000 blocks of E. U.S. 350 in Raytown and Raytown Rd. and 63rd St. Everything from pizza and chicken to burgers and steak can be found along these busy corridors.

Fast Food Havens, west of U.S. 71 on Blue Ridge Blvd. The section swings around Truman Corners shopping center and features burgers, tacos, pizza and more.

GOODIES

Our Doll Land, 5th St. and M-291 (3 blocks north of U.S. 350 on M-291), Lee's Summit, MO 64063, 525-7610. This store is known for its delicious homemade fudge that comes in a dozen different flavors including peanut butter and rocky road. The place also carries collectible dolls, bears, toys and gifts.

BELTON-RAYMORE, MISSOURI

Convention Bureaus and Chambers of Commerce

Belton Chamber of Commerce, 605 Cherry St., Belton, MO 64012, 331-2420.

Raymore Chamber of Commerce, City Hall, 210 S. Washington, Box 885, Raymore, MO 64083, 322-0599.

Clubs and Organizations

YMCA Of Greater Kansas City. (See Clubs and Organizations, Midtown, Kansas City, MO)

Special Assistance for the Disabled

Cass County Reserve-A-Ride, 200 W. Wall, Harrisonville, MO 64701, 816-884-4390. Service is provided for seniors and the physically disabled for Cass County, Independence, and Kansas City on request.

Parks and Recreation Departments

Belton Parks and Recreation, Commercial and Pine Sts., Belton, MO 64012, 331-0336.

BUSINESS AND COMMERCIAL TOURS

Galaxy Farms, 2501 W. Foxwood Dr. (M-58, 1 mile E. of U.S. 71), Raymore, MO 64083, 331-1116. This horse farm provides tours of the barn where quarter, saddle, and Arabian horses are kept. *Time Frame:* 30 minutes up. *Ages:* all. *Important to Know:* (I/R) (G/R) (No $) (B)

HISTORIC SITES AND MUSEUMS

City Hall Museum, 512 Main St., Belton, MO 64012, 331-4454. Housed in the old original Belton City Hall, this museum features Indian artifacts and arrows from pioneer days. Kids can see exhibits about famous personalities like Harry S. Truman. *Time Frame:* 30 minutes. *Ages:* all. *Important to Know:* (I) (G/R) ($) (B)

AMUSEMENTS

Kountry Kids Bat and Putt, 8312 E. 171st St. (M-58, 1 block E. of Walmart), Belton, MO 64012, 322-2340. This facility has four batting cages, a miniature golf course, video arcade and concessions. *Ages:* tots up. *Important to Know:* family night special and team/group rates available. ($) (B)

THE GREAT OUTDOORS

Special Area Parks and Playgrounds

The following parks offer ballfields, tennis courts, picnic areas and more. They have bathrooms.

Raymore Memorial Park, Olive St. and Park Dr., Raymore, MO 64083, 331-0488.

Belton Memorial Park, Commercial St., Belton, MO 64012, 331-0336.

SPECIAL LIBRARY PROGRAMS

Cass County Public Library, Belton Branch, 422 Main, Belton, MO 64012, 331-0049. Summer reading programs, films and story hours are available.

Cass County Public Library, Raymore Branch, 112 N. Madison, Raymore, MO 64083, 331-8024. Summer reading programs, films and story hours offered. (D)

CLAY COUNTY, MISSOURI

KANSAS CITY, NORTH KANSAS CITY, CLAYCOMO, GLADSTONE, KEARNEY, EXCELSIOR SPRINGS, SMITHVILLE LAKE, AND LIBERTY

KEY: (I) individual tours, no reservations needed; (I/R) indi-vidual tours, reservations needed; (G) group tours, no reser-vations needed; (G/R) group tours, reservations needed; ($) fee; (No $) no fee; (B) bathrooms; (No B) no bathrooms; (D) some accommodations for the disabled.

KANSAS CITY, NORTH KANSAS CITY, CLAYCOMO, GLADSTONE

ASSISTANCE

(NOTE: All Missouri phone numbers have an 816 area code prefix)

Convention Bureaus and Chambers of Commerce

Northland Chamber of Commerce, 1806 Swift Avenue, North Kansas City, MO 64116, 221-0233.

City Hall, North Kansas City, 2010 Howell St., North Kansas City, MO 64116, 274-6000.

Gladstone Chamber of Commerce, 7001 N. Locust, Gladstone, MO 64118, 436-3400.

Clubs and Organizations

Mid-Continent Council of Girl Scouts (See Assistance, East of Plaza, Kansas City, MO.)

Kansas City, Missouri, Council of Camp Fire. (See Assistance, East of Plaza, Kansas City, MO.)

Heart of America Council, Boy Scouts of America. (See Assistance, Kansas City, KS.)

Clay-Platte YMCA, 1101 N.E. 47th St., Kansas City, MO 64116, 453-6600. The YMCA has an abundance of sports and cultural programs for kids, plus day camps, child care, and other offerings. Rather than trying to list them all in our limited space, we suggest calling for more information.

Special Assistance—Day Care

Division of Family Services. (See Assistance, Downtown, Kansas City, MO.)

Clay-Platte Branch YWCA, 2700 Buchanan, North Kansas City, MO 64116, 221-2767.

Special Assistance for the Disabled

Clay-Platte Association for Retarded Citizens, Inc., 7211 N. Broadway, Gladstone, MO 64118, 436-1704. The organization benefits Clay-Platte residents who are mentally or physically impaired. It offers a pre-school program for children, infants through K, plus a summer day camp for youngsters ages 6 to 21. It also supports area Special Olympics and a bowling league for the disabled.

Concerned Care, Inc., 1509 N.E. Parvin Rd., Kansas City, MO 64116, 455-3026. (Also see Outdoor Education, this section.) Primarily a residential program for adults, Concerned Care also has an active recreation program for retarded persons of all ages, and a summer day camp for young people ages 6 to 21.

**Direction Service Center, 1511 Kingshighway, Indepen-
dence, MO 64055, 833-4415.** (See Listing under Special
Assistance for the Disabled, Independence, MO.) This
organization publishes a pamphlet featuring summer programs for disabled children.

**The Whole Person, Inc., 6301 Rockhill Rd., Suite 305E,
Kansas City, MO 64131, 361-0304 (VOICE), 361-7749 (TTY).**
(See Listing under Special Assistance for the Disabled,
South of Plaza, Kansas City, MO.) This is a private not-for-
profit organization for people with disabilities.

Transportation

Kansas City Area Transportation Authority, 221-0660.

Parks and Recreation Departments

*Because of space limitations, it's impossible for us to list the
wealth of children's outdoor, sports, and cultural programs
offered by area parks and recreation. Some departments
also have "Pre School Parents Day Out" itineraries. We*

suggest calling the appropriate division for brochures and information about their individual schedules.

Gladstone Parks and Recreation Dept., 7010 N. Holmes, Gladstone, MO 64118, 436-2200.

Kansas City, Missouri, Parks and Recreation Department, 5605 E. 63rd St., Kansas City, MO 64130, 444-3113. (See Listings under The Great Outdoors, Kansas City, MO, Jackson County.)

North Kansas City Parks and Recreation Department, 2010 Howell St., North Kansas City, MO 64116, 274-6008.

BUSINESS AND COMMERCIAL TOURS

Fins and Foliage Pet Store, 7022 N. Locust, Gladstone, MO 64118, 436-6062. Kids can play with a puppy, pet a guinea pig, tour a fish room, and talk to the birds on the educational tour of this large pet store. Questions are encouraged. *Time Frame:* 15 minutes. *Ages:* Preschool on up. *Important to Know:* (G/R) (No $) (B) (D)

Ford Motor Company, U.S. 69, Claycomo, MO 64119, 459-1348. This walking tour takes visitors through a passenger vehicle product system to see how cars and trucks are made. *Time Frame:* one hour. *Ages:* 1st grade up. *Important to Know:* wear comfortable shoes. (G/R) (No $) (B)

Hunt Midwest Enterprises, Inc., 8300 N.E. Underground Dr., Kansas City, MO 64161, 455-2500. The public is welcome to drive through this huge underground storage area and Foreign Trade Zone located inside manmade, limestone caves. There is no formal tour here, but you can see the business area during the week. Stay in your car; no walking outside is allowed. *Important to Know:* (No $) (No B)

Jessica's Cookies, Metro North Mall, 400 N.W. Barry Rd., Kansas City, MO 64118, 436-1906. A tour through this sweet place teaches children how cookies are made, baked and then frozen. Each child is given a "cookie pop" to decorate.

Time Frame: 30 minutes. *Ages:* K through 6th grade. *Important to Know:* (G/R) ($) (B)

Kansas City, Missouri, Water Treatment Plant,
1 N.W. Briarcliff Rd., Kansas City, MO 64116, 454-6233. Kids see a 30-minute movie on how Missouri River water is pumped, then treated and distributed. They'll get a tour of the laboratory, pump area and control room as well as a brochure of fun facts explaining how water is made potable. *Time Frame:* 1½ hours. *Ages:* 2nd grade up. *Important to Know:* (I/R) (G/R) (No $) (B)

Northland Mobile Veterinarian Clinic, 4207 N. Colorado, Kansas City, MO 64117, 223-1772. Children learn about
basic animal medical care as they tour the clinic. There's a short movie about rabies and a question-and-answer period to discuss pet care. This helps kids learn about the responsibilities of owning a pet. *Time Frame:* an hour. *Ages:* 3rd through 6th grade. *Important to Know:* (G/R) (No $) (No B)

North Kansas City Hospital, 2800 Hospital Drive,
Kansas City, MO 64116, 346-7000. The tour familiarizes youngsters with hospital procedures, lab work, surgery and hospital rooms. After a short slide show, "Dandy-Lion" makes an appearance. Cookies, punch and surgical masks are passed out as souvenirs of the occasion. *Time Frame:* 45 minutes. *Ages:* preschool through 12 years. *Important to Know:* (G/R) (No $) (B) (D)

Dr. Victor E. Rodman, D.D.S, Pediatric Specialist,
231 N.W. 72, Gladstone, MO 64118, 436-5900. This is a painless dental visit, complete with a Peanuts movie about dentistry. Kids can find out how all the machinery works, try out the chair and look at X-rays. At the end of the tour, youngsters get a free tooth decay prevention packet complete with toothbrush and dental floss. *Time Frame:* 30 minutes. *Ages:* Age 7 and under. *Important to Know:* (I/R) (G/R) (No $) (B) (D)

Show Biz Pizza, Antioch Mall, 2726 N.E. Vivion Rd.,
Kansas City, MO 64119, 452-7533. The step by step process of pizza making, from rolling out the dough to baking it, is part of this tour for kids. The price include a look at the kitchen, one large pizza cut into 16 slices, 6 drinks and 25

tokens for the restaurant's video games. *Time Frame:* 30 minutes for the tour. *Ages:* 6 up. *Important to Know:* (G/R) ($) (B)

Townsend Communications, Inc., 7007 N.E. Parvin Rd., Kansas City, MO 64117, 454-9660. TCI, which publishes the Dispatch-Tribune newspapers and other publications, holds tours of their editorial offices. Children can meet the staff, visit advertising and production areas, and watch the presses at work. *Time Frame:* 30 minutes. *Ages:* The tour is advisable for older children, since kids under age 7 may be bored with the various phases involved in printing. *Important to Know:* (G/R) (No $) (B)

THE ARTS

Young Audiences Arts Card, Kansas City Chapter of Young Audiences™ (See The Arts, Midtown, Kansas City, MO.)

First Gallery, First Bank of Gladstone, 7001 N. Oak Trafficway, Gladstone, MO 64118, 436-1900. Older children may like viewing the gallery in the southeast wing of the bank. March brings local work by junior and senior high school students. It's a hassle-free way to gently expose kids to art. *Important to Know:* (No $) (B) (D)

Gladstone Oak Grove Theater In The Park, 76th and N. Troost, P.O. Box 10719, Gladstone, MO 64118, 436-2200. This endeavor provides a family-type stage production once a year in Oak Grove Park. Most productions have children in the cast. If youngsters get bored, there's playground equipment, a picnic area, and fishing pond nearby. *Time Frame:* performances run about two hours. *Ages:* all. *Important to Know:* bring something to sit on. (No $) (B)

Northgate Community Theater, Northgate Community Education Center, 2117 N.E. 48th St., Kansas City, MO 64117, 454-PLAY. This family-oriented theater puts on three productions a year, plus a children's Christmas show that's performed in malls and for large groups. *Time Frame:* performances run about two hours; the Christmas show, about 45 minutes. *Ages:* 2nd grade up. *Important to Know:* ($) (B) (D)

AMUSEMENTS

Fantasyland Roller Rink and Miniature Golf, 6970 N. Broadway (68th St. exit E. off U.S. 169), Gladstone, MO 64118, 436-6060, 436-9556. This popular place features a skating rink, miniature golf course and batting cages. Skating lessons are available. *Ages:* tots up. *Important to Know:* ($) (B)

North Kansas City Pro Bowl, Mini Golf and Go-Cart Track, 505 E. 18th Ave., North Kansas City, MO 64116, 221-8844. Lots of other amusements are offered at this same location including a video arcade and snack bar. *Ages:* all. *Important to Know:* ($) (B)

Sherwood Family Recreation Center, 4900 N. Norton, Kansas City, MO 64119, 452-4457. Owned by the Sherwood Bible Church, the family-oriented facility is not restricted to church members and offers lighted tennis courts, volleyball and basketball courts, and an Olympic size pool. There's a swimming team and tennis lessons for all ages. *Ages:* all. *Important to Know:* no smoking or alcohol is allowed on the premises. Women must wear one-piece swimwear. Headphones must be used with radios. ($) (B)

Oceans of Fun, Exit 54 off I-435, adjacent to Worlds of Fun, Kansas City, MO 64161, 459-WAVE. This 60-acre amusement park features a wave pool, water slides, beaches, games, boating and entertainment. *Ages:* all. *Important to Know:* dressing facilities and showers available. Bring lots of towels, sunscreen and sunglasses. Passes are available in combination with Worlds of Fun. Special group rates. ($) (B)

Worlds of Fun, I-435 and Parvin Road, 4545 Worlds of Fun Ave., Kansas City, MO 64161, 454-4444. This popular family amusement park packs nearly 160 acres with exciting rides and live entertainment. Geared for all ages it has a variety of attractions from the sensational "Python Plunge" to the "Pandamonium" pint-size adventures for tots. *Ages:* all. *Important to Know:* you can rent strollers, lockers and cameras here, and park the pets in a free kennel. Wear sun screen and comfortable shoes. Weekends are crowded.

Group and senior citizen discounts offered. Children under 3 are free. ($) (B) (D)

SPORTS

Kansas City Pro Bowl, 505 E. 18th Ave., North Kansas City, MO 64116, 221-8844. The Pro Bowl has Saturday morning children's leagues for ages 6 to 18. Also offered on Saturday mornings: Baby Bumpers for kids 3 to 5. Billiards, video games, snack bar, batting range, go-carts and miniature golf round out the fare. The Pro Bowl is located next door to the Gold Buffet restaurant. *Important to Know:* ($) (B)

Kansas City North Community Center Sports Programs, 3930 N.E. Antioch Rd., Kansas City, MO 64117, 452-7244. The center features seasonal soccer, tennis, basketball and volleyball, and judo after school and on Saturdays. Funded by Kansas City, MO, Parks and Recreation, the program also offers a Kiddie Club, piano and exercise lessons. *Ages:* vary, according to sport. *Important to Know:* ($) (B) (D)

King Louie Bowling Center, Northland Lanes, I-29 and Vivion Rd., Kansas City, MO 64118, 454-2695. Junior league games are offered on Saturday mornings for children. The center also has video games and billiards. *Ages:* 5 up. *Important to Know:* ($) (B) (D)

Public Swimming Pool, 5501 Scandia Lane, in the Scandia Village Apartment area, Kansas City, MO 274-1671. Other public pools include Gladstone Municipal Swimming Pool, 70th and North Holmes, Gladstone, MO, 436-2299; and North Kansas City Municipal Swimming Pool, 2201 Howell, North Kansas City, MO, 842-8400. Open to families and individuals. *Important to Know:* ($) (B)

PLAYING TOGETHER

Gladstone Bowl, 300 W. 72nd St., North, Gladstone, MO 64118, 436-2695. Two nights a week the center hosts a youth-adult league so that parents and their children can bowl together. Children's bowling leagues are also offered. *Ages:* 4 to 18. *Important to Know:* ($) (B)

Northland Pre-School Parents Club, 1000 N.E. 86th St., Kansas City, MO 64155, 436-5125. Formed in 1974, this club provides a newsletter and activities for preschoolers and their parents. Several monthly outings are planned including field trips and art classes. This is a great way to explore the city with your child and take advantage of group events not normally offered to individuals. *Ages:* pre-schoolers and parents. *Important to Know:* membership is open to all Northland families. ($)

Northgate Community Education Center Youth Classes, Northgate Community Center, 2117 N.E. 48th St., Kansas City, MO 64118, 453-2250. Classes such as Jumping Jax exercise and Learning Through Play are open to toddlers and their parents. *Ages:* 2 up. *Important to Know:* ($) (B)

THE GREAT OUTDOORS

Special Programs and Exhibits

Hodge Park Heritage Village, 7000 N.E. Barry Rd. (North of M-152, between I-435 and I-35), send mail to 5940 N.W. Waukomis, Kansas City, MO 64151, 444-4363. This reconstructed village features authentic pioneer log cabin homes, a grist mill, plantation estate, school house, church, jail, and general store. There are fenced areas of buffalo and elk nearby. The village is located in a 629-acre park which has a public golf course, picnic sites, baseball diamonds and more. *Ages:* all. *Important to Know:* Open in summer. (No $) (B)

Heritage Village Mini-Workshops, 7000 N.E. Barry Rd., send mail to 5940 N.W. Waukomis, Kansas City, MO 64151, 444-4363. Each summer Heritage Village holds weekend classes in pioneer crafts. Everything from wood-carving and run-braiding to scrimshaw and basket-making is offered. *Ages:* 10 up. *Important to Know:* ($) (B)

Special Area Parks and Playgrounds

Most area parks offer picnic areas, ball fields, tennis courts, playgrounds, shelters and more. The Parks and Recreation Department also provides "Open-Door" after-school programs at some schools (274-1671). For more information call: Gladstone Parks and Recreation Dept., 436-2200; North Kansas City Parks and Recreation, 274-6008; or Kansas City, Missouri, Parks and Recreation, 444-4363.

Central Park, 69th and N. Holmes, Gladstone, MO. Has a public swimming pool. The Gladstone Teachers Memorial, near the pool area, holds a special monument honoring teachers, including Space Shuttle Challenger's special passenger, Christa McAuliffe.

Chaumiere Woods Park, just off N. 43rd St. and N. Indiana St., Kansas City, MO. Has a fishing lake. Ducks and geese that live on the lake are tame enough for children to feed. This is a small park, but because it's close to I-35, it's a convenient stop for families who want to get close to nature without having to drive a long distance. It's close to a gas station and a convenience store.

Dagg Park, 21st and Howell St., North Kansas City, MO.

Englewood Park, Englewood Rd. and N. Troost, Kansas City, MO. Has a fishing lake. Saturdays are crowded. Watch the kids around the lake. Swimming is not allowed.

Golden Oaks Park, N. 46th St. and N. Antioch Rd., Kansas City, MO. This is close to Antioch Shopping Center.

Happy Rock Park, 76th St. and N. Antioch Rd., Gladstone, MO. The park has nature trails.

Hidden Valley Park, N.E. Parvin Rd. and N. Bennington Ave., Kansas City, MO. There is a nature trail through a heavily wooded area.

Hodge Park, 7000 N.E. Barry Rd. (M-152), Kansas City, MO. The largest park north of the river, Hodge Park features an 18-hole golf course, an enclosure for buffalo and elk, and Heritage Village, an 1850's reconstruction of a pioneer town.

Hobby Hill Park, 76th Terr. and North Main, Gladstone, MO. Here you'll find a nature trail and a natural spring.

Lakewood Greenway (Penguin Park), Vivion Rd. and N. Norton, Kansas City, MO. Huge fiberglas animals dot the playground here including a supersize kangaroo and elephant. In winter the park is converted to Santa's Wonderland. The park has a fishing lake and woods and is conveniently located on the main drag of Vivion Rd. Look for the giant penguin.

Macken Park, 716 E. 27th Ave., North Kansas City, MO. This large park is perfect for a picnic or family reunion. Reserve a shelter by calling 274-6008.

Northgate Park, Davidson Rd. and N.E. 46th Terr., Kansas City, MO. The park contains Northland's only public fountain which freezes over in winter, creating a fascinating ice sculpture that changes with the weather. The water is also sometimes colored. The park is flanked on three sides by busy roads, so watch the kids. There's a plenty of shopping and eating nearby on North Oak Trafficway.

Oak Grove Park, 76th and North Troost, Gladstone, MO. Has a fishing pond and is noted for the picturesque fall foliage provided by its 150-year-old oak trees.

Waterworks Park, 3200 N. Oak Trafficway, Kansas City, MO. There's a scenic view here that overlooks the city.

Nature Sanctuaries

Maple Woods Nature Preserve, N. Prospect and N.E. 72nd St., Gladstone, MO 64118, 436-2200. A pristine forest, this nature preserve is the largest stand of sugar maples west of the Mississippi River. About 45 acres hold deer, raccoons, skunks, possums, birds and bugs. There are six miles of nature trails to roam. *Ages:* all. *Important to Know:* (No $) (No B)

Outdoor Education Programs

Concerned Care Day Camp, 1509 N.E. Parvin Rd., Kansas City, MO 64116, 455-3026. This supervised summer program for mentally retarded kids provides crafts, arts and nature projects, singing, musical entertainment and more. *Ages:* 6 to 21. *Important to Know:* ($) (D)

Summer Discovery Program, Macken Park, 27th and Howell, North Kansas City, MO 64116, 274-6008. Sponsored by North Kansas City Parks and Recreation Department, the weekday morning activities include games, sports, crafts, music, drama and special events and a "Summer Tot Program." *Ages:* Pre-schooler to 12. *Important to Know:* flexible summer hours. ($) (D)

Summer Camping Programs

Y-Land, 2700 Buchanan St., North Kansas City, MO 64116, 221-2767. The day camp offers field trips, swimming lessons, art, science, and sport classes, games, puppetry and dramatics. The hours are perfect for working parents with school-age children and the price is cheaper than paying a babysitter to watch the kids during the summer. *Ages:* 5 to 12. *Important to Know:* ($)

SPECIAL LIBRARY PROGRAMS

Many Northland libraries have programs such as a story hour or films for pre-schoolers and elementary school-age children. Call the library nearest you for information. Some places to start include:

Mid-Continent Library, Gladstone Branch, 6565 N. Oak Trafficway, Gladstone, MO 64118, 436-4385.

North Kansas City Public Library, 715 E. 23rd Ave., North Kansas City, MO 64116, 331-3360.

Mid-Continent Library, Antioch Branch, 6060 N. Chestnut, Kansas City, MO 64119, 454-1306.

SPECIAL ACTIVITIES

Friday on the Square, in Town Square at Armour and Swift in downtown North Kansas City, MO 64116, 274-6000. Each Friday in May from 11:30 a.m. to 1 p.m., this City of North Kansas City-sponsored event provides free music and entertainment to the public. It's a great place to have lunch and bring the kids. *Important to Know:* (No $) (B)

Kansas City North Community Center, 3930 N.E. Antioch Rd., Kansas City, MO 64117, 452-7244. The center holds year-around children's classes offering arts and crafts, music lessons, gymnastics and more. *Ages:* pre-school through 15. *Important to Know:* lessons are after school during the week; leagues are on Saturdays. *Important to Know:* ($) (B) (D—ramp in back of center).

Northland Mothers of Twins Club, c/o Kellie Olsen, 5507 N.W. Meadowvale, Kansas City, MO 64151, 587-9908.

This is a support group and social club for mothers of twins and multiples and expectant moms. The group meets monthly and has family activities several times a year including Halloween and Christmas parties. *Important to Know:* all metro area moms welcome.

Northgate Community Education Center Youth Classes, Northgate Community Center, 2117 N.E. 48th St., Kansas City, MO 64118, 453-2250. (Also see Playing Together.) Spring and fall classes offer dance, tennis, tumbling, baton twirling, and some parent-child exercise and play classes. *Ages:* 2 up. *Important to Know:* ($) (B)

Youth Enrichment Program, Maple Woods Community College, 2601 N.E. Barry Rd., Kansas City, MO 64156, 436-6500, Ext. 190. A program of summer classes is offered for children featuring topics ranging from cartooning and aviation to geology and computers. *Ages:* grades 1 to 12. *Important to Know:* ($) (B) (D)

SPECIAL EVENTS CALENDAR

MARCH

Snake Saturday, City of North Kansas City, 2010 Howell St., North Kansas City, MO 64116, 274-6000. This family-oriented Irish celebration is held in downtown North Kansas City the Saturday before St. Patrick's Day. Money raised is donated to charities. The main focus is a late morning parade that draws thousands of people, followed by entertainment throughout the afternoon. There's a petting zoo and free cartoons for kids, as well as games, children's contests and a Moonwalk. *Important to Know:* (No $)

JUNE

Frontier Festival, Hodge Park, 7000 N.E. Barry Rd., sponsored by Kansas City Parks and Recreation Department and Assistance League of Kansas City Northland, 5605 E. 63rd St., Kansas City, MO 64130, 444-4363. The day-long event is held in Heritage Village the first Saturday in June. It features 19th Century games for kids, a watermelon-eating contest and more. Pioneer crafts, such as spinning, candle-making, and wood-carving are demonstrated. *Important to Know:* (No $)

SEPTEMBER

Northtown Fall Festival, City of North Kansas City, North Kansas City Merchants Assn., 2010 Howell St., North Kansas City, MO 64116, 274-6000. Held in downtown North Kansas City, at the intersection of Armour and Swift, the annual event includes an arts and crafts show, live entertainment, and food, with pony rides and games for children. *Important to Know:* (No $ to get in)

OCTOBER

Gladfest, Gladstone Chamber of Commerce, 7001 Locust St., Gladstone, MO 64118, 436-3400. A parade, arts and crafts show, games, and a barbecue are part of the fun, plus there's a carnival with games and rides for the kids. *Important to Know:* (No $)

FUN EATS

Perkins, 6292 N. Oak Trafficway, Kansas City, MO 64118, 452-3650. (Check your phone book for other Perkins locations around Greater Kansas City.) The children's menu here features everything from burgers to pancakes, plus desserts.

Stroud's Oak Ridge Manor, 5410 N.E. Oak Ridge Dr., Kansas City, MO 64119, 454-9600. The popular restaurant serves its famous fried chicken and cinnamon rolls family-style. A children's menu is available. (D)

Showbiz Pizza Palace, 2726 N.E. Vivion Rd., Antioch Shopping Center, Kansas City, MO 64119, 454-4888. (Check your phone book for other Showbiz Pizza locations around Greater Kansas City.) This popular family place has pizza, hot dogs, a salad bar and stage show, plus a game room with kiddie rides, ski ball, and videos. Birthday packages require advance reservations. (D)

Tippins Restaurant and Pie Pantry, 5080 N. Oak Trafficway, Kansas City, MO 64118, 459-7550. (Check your phone book for other Tippins restaurant locations around Greater Kansas City.) Besides luscious pies, Tippins has a menu for all age groups. (D)

Fast Food Havens, the 6000 block of N.E. Antioch Rd., the 4000 to 8000 blocks of N. Oak Trafficway, the 2000 block of N.E. Vivion Rd. around Antioch Shopping Center, and the 1200 block of Armour in North Kansas City. These are just a few of the areas which offer everything from restaurants serving seafood, barbecue and steaks to pizza, hamburgers, chicken and more.

KEARNEY AND EXCELSIOR SPRINGS

HISTORIC SITES AND MUSEUMS

Mount Gilead School, Kearney, MO., contact Clay County Parks and Recreation Historic Sites, 103 N. Water St., Liberty, MO 64068, 816-635-6065. This one-room schoolhouse remained open during the Civil War. The county schedules an actual day-long class complete with a "school marm," and McGuffey's Readers. The session is taught as if it were 100 years ago: instruction is given in reading, penmanship, history and spelling. A 38-star American flag flies in front. *Time Frame:* all day. *Ages:* 3rd and 4th grades. *Important to Know:* open only to school groups. Let your school district know this activity is available. (No $) (B)

Claybrook House Historic Site, West of Jesse James Farm on M-92, 2 miles east of Kearney, MO 64065, 816-635-6055. This pre-Civil War plantation-style residence was built in 1858. It was the home of Jesse James' daughter, Mary James-Barr. Claybrook and the nearby Jesse James farm will give children a look at how the rich and poor lived during the same time period. In summer there are Civil War re-enactments on the grounds. *Time Frame:* 30 minutes. *Ages:* 8 up. *Important to Know:* this is farm country. Wear comfy shoes and bring a picnic basket and make this a Day Trip since you're within easy reach of the James Farm, Watkins Mill State Park, and Tryst Falls. Claybrook is open May to September. (I) (G/R) ($) (B)

Jesse James Farm and Visitors Center, 2 miles E. of Kearney on M-92, Rt. 2, Box 236, Kearney, MO 64065, 816-635-6065. Built in 1822, this farm was the boyhood home of outlaws Jesse and Frank James, the sons of a Baptist minister. Restoration of the home includes original furnishings and artifacts. Children are usually interested in the personal effects such as guns, clothing, and books. They'll also learn how common folks lived during the Civil War era. The home is open to tour year-around and the guided tours give a fascinating history of the outlaws. *Time Frame:* about an hour. *Ages:* 6 up. *Important to Know:* a ticket to the farm will get you in free to Claybrook House down the road in summer. (I) (G/R) ($) (B)

Watkins Woolen Mill State Historic Site, 6½ miles north of Excelsior Springs and 1½ miles W. of Country Rd. MM in Lawson, MO 64062, 816-296-3357. (Also see Kearney, The Great Outdoors.) This is the last 19th Century textile mill in America with the original equipment. The Watkins home is also on site. In 1861 children worked in the mill from morning until night. The windows were never opened and the temperature soared to over 100 degrees. That information, plus the fact that cookies and goodies are made on the kitchen woodstove here on weekends, should interest kids. *Time Frame:* about an hour. *Ages:* 1st grade up. *Important to Know:* Bring comfy shoes. Once the tour is through, you can spend a warm weather day hiking, biking, fishing or swimming in the park. (I) (G/R) ($) (B)

Jesse James Grave, Mount Olivet Cemetery, west end of M-92, on your way out of Kearney. Jesse's grave is located under a big cedar tree on the cemetery's west side. Originally he was buried on the front lawn of the farm, so that his family could protect his remains from grave robbers and curiosity seekers. For years Jesse's mother, Zerelda, sold pebbles off the grave to tourists. Later his body was moved to Mount Olivet.

THE GREAT OUTDOORS

Special Programs and Exhibits

Watkins Mill State Park, 6 miles north of Excelsior Springs, off M-92 and Highway RA, in Lawson, MO 64062, 816-296-3387. (Also see Kearney Historic Sites and Museums.) Watkins Woolen Mill State Historic Site is adjacent to this 1,300-acre state park which features picnicking, camping, hiking or swimming in the lake. Bring your bike along and enjoy the bike/hike trail around the shore line. Campsites available. *Ages:* all. *Important to Know:* bring food and drink since there are no concessions here. (No $) (B)

Special Area Parks and Playgrounds

Tryst Falls Park, M-92, 5 miles E. of Kearney and I-35, near Kearney, MO., 532-0803. Clay County Parks and Recreation runs this 40-acre park which includes the area's only waterfall open to the public. Picnicking, tennis and fishing are also offered. Jesse James' father, a Baptist minister, baptised Walthus Watkins, owner of Watkins Mill, at Tryst Falls. *Important to Know:* Swimming is dangerous here because of the rocks and is not allowed. The park makes a sightseeing stop in your tour of Jesse James Farm or Watkins Mill State Park. (No $) (No B)

SPECIAL ACTIVITIES

"The Life and Times of Jesse James," Clay County Dept. of Parks, Recreation and Historic Sites, James Farm, 2 miles E. of Kearney on M-92, Kearney, MO 64065, 816-532-0654. (For information write Clay County Parks and Recreation Dept., Rte. 2, Box 120, Smithville, MO 64089.) This original 3-act play about Jesse James is performed August through early September on the front lawn of the Jesse James home. The professional production packs plenty of action, with gunfights, a hanging, fire bombs and galloping horses. If kids get fidgety, there's lots of outdoor room to run around. *Time Frame:* about 2 hours. *Ages:* 3rd grade up. *Important to Know:* Refreshments and stadium seating are available ($) (B)

The Elms Resort and Conference Center, Regent and Elms Blvd., Excelsior Springs, MO 64024, 781-8600, 1-800-843-3567. If a family weekend away from home intrigues you, the Elms has a wealth of things to do for kids including Bingo, Trivial Pursuit, a Coketail party for teens, and a children's dinner party where youngsters can eat together and play games afterward. Plus there are a variety of sports and other activities to keep young ones entertained. *Ages:* 4 to 17. *Important to Know:* (I/R) ($) (B) (D)

SPECIAL EVENTS

Jesse James Days, sponsored by the Jesse James Festival Committee, Inc., P.O. Box 536, Kearney, MO 64060, 816-635-4142. A parade, music, craft show, entertainment, and outlaw shootouts provide family fun for all. Held on a mid-September weekend. *Important to Know:* (I) (G) (No $) (B)

SMITHVILLE LAKE

THE GREAT OUTDOORS

Special Programs and Exhibits

Smithville Lake, Jerry L. Litton Visitor Center, State Highway DD, southwest end of dam, Smithville, MO 64089, 532-0174. Named after the late 6th District Congressman, the center offers exhibits and artifacts on the Missouri Valley and the Indians who inhabited it. There's information on 7,200-acre Smithville Lake and dam, and the life of Litton. The center also has nature films and tours of the dam control tower on summer weekends. *Ages:* 1st grade up. *Important to Know:* (No $) (B)

Smithville Lake and Clay County Parks, (Camp Branch, Little Platte Park, and Crow's Creek Campground) 2 miles east of U.S. 169 on N.E. 180th St., Smithville, MO 64089, 532-0803. The 7,200-acre lake features two swimming beaches, a hiking trail, playgrounds, campground, marinas with boat rentals, camping and picnic sites, and a visitors center. Kids can swim, fish, and play all day. *Ages:* all. *Important to Know:* weekends are most crowded. No lifeguards on duty. Shelter houses available by reservation. ($) (B) (D—facilities at Crows Creek, Camp Branch, and Smith's Fork)

Smithville Lake—Woodhenge, west side of lake, Smithville, MO 64089, 792-2221. This is a working replica of the only known square prehistoric Indian solar calendar.

The original site was flooded when Smithville Lake was created. It's an interesting place to take children if you're already at the lake. *Ages:* 8 up. *Important to Know:* ($) (B— in the park)

Summer Camping Programs

Day Camp at Smithville Lake, headquartered at the Clay-Platte Branch of YMCA, 1101 N.E. 47th St., Kansas City, MO 64116, 453-6600. This program runs weekdays in the summer and includes nature study, field and canoe trips, archery, arts and crafts and more. It's held at Smithville Lake, which affords access to sand beaches, woods, nature trails and shoreline. *Ages:* 6 to 12. *Important to Know:* ($) (B)

LIBERTY

ASSISTANCE

Convention Bureaus and Chambers of Commerce

Clay County Visitors Bureau, Clay County Administration Building, Courthouse Square, Liberty, MO 64068, 792-7691.

Liberty Chamber of Commerce, 109 S. Leonard St., Liberty, MO 64068, 781-5200.

Transportation

Mayflower Contract Services, P.O. Box 7941, Shawnee Mission, KS 66207, 345-1986. The company operates routes in Excelsior Springs and Liberty weekly. The company provides service to Royals Games from Kansas City North area. Children 5 and under ride free.

Kansas City Area Transportation Authority, 221-0660.

Parks and Recreation Departments

Liberty Parks and Recreation Dept., 101 E. Kansas St., Liberty, MO 64068, 781-7100, Ext. 218. Phone for information on their special sports programs for kids.

BUSINESS AND COMMERCIAL TOURS

Liberty Hospital, 2525 Glenn Hendren Drive, Liberty, MO 64068, 781-7200. The child's favorite teddy bear can be used as the patient, as the youngster goes through Emergency Room procedures at the "Teddy Bear Clinic." From there the kids tour different hospital departments including the pediatrics ward. *Time Frame:* an hour. *Ages:* 3 to 6. *Important to Know:* (No $) (B) (D)

James A. Rooney Justice Center, Clay County Courthouse, 11 S. Water, Liberty, MO 64068, 792-7612. The newly constructed courthouse offers outdoor ceramic murals depicting the county's history. If the court is in session, children may sit in, but they must be *quiet*. This is a self-guided tour. *Time Frame:* 30 minutes or less. *Ages:* 2nd grade up. *Important to Know:* this is an easy way to acquaint children with the legal system. (I) (G) (No $) (B) (D)

HISTORIC SITES AND MUSEUMS

There are several historical buildings on the square in Liberty and others within walking distance such as Boggess Hardware on Kansas St. on the south side of the square, with its old tin ceiling and wooden floors and the murals at the James Rooney Justice Center. Other structures of note include:

Clay County Museum, 14 N. Main, Liberty, MO 64068, 781-8062. Housed in a drugstore that opened in 1865, the museum features a restored doctor's office. Kids will especially enjoy seeing the prehistoric Indian relics, toys, tools, arrowheads, and old doctor's equipment. Some exhibits offer taped recordings about the items displayed. *Time Frame:* 30 minutes. *Ages:* 2nd grade up. *Important to Know:* (I) (G/R) (No $) (No B)

Jessee James Bank Museum and Historic Site,
N.E. corner of Courthouse Square (103 N. Water St.),
Liberty, MO 64068, 781-4458. Here's where Jesse and Frank
James made the first successful daylight bank robbery in
history (during peacetime) on Feb. 13, 1866. A guided tour
takes visitors through this authentically restored building.
The presentation gives details about gold, banking, what old
money looked like and, of course, provides a glimpse into
the lives of these famed outlaws. Once the tour ends you can
eat next door at the Crawford House, a fine restaurant
located in an old funeral home. Get dessert. *Time Frame:* 30
minutes. *Ages:* 1st grade up. *Important to Know:* (I) (G/R)
($) (B)

Historic Liberty Jail and Visitors Center (Mormon
Jail), 216 N. Main St., Liberty, MO 64068, 781-3188. This is
where Mormon leader, Joseph Smith, was imprisoned in
1838 for his beliefs. Built in 1833, the limestone jail eventually
crumbled but was reconstructed by the Church of Jesus
Christ of Latter-Day Saints in 1963. The jail has cutaway

walls so kids can see what conditions were like a century ago. It also teaches children about the unfairness of persecution of those whose faith may be different from their own. *Time Frame:* 30-45 minutes. *Ages:* 2nd grade up. *Important to Know:* (G/R) (No $) (B)

Lightburne Hall, 301 N. Water St., Liberty, MO 64068, 781-5567. Built in 1852, this large, brick plantation mansion is an excellent example of antebellum-style architecture. Older children might like seeing the old-time furnishings. If they've seen "Gone With The Wind," they'll get a kick out of the large portrait of "Scarlet O'Hara" which hangs in the dining room. This is a private residence open for tours by appointment only. *Time Frame:* 30 minutes or less. *Ages:* 8 up. *Important to Know:* (I/R) (G/R) ($) (B)

THE ARTS

Young Audiences Art Card, Kansas City Chapter of Young Audiences. (See the Arts, Midtown Kansas City, MO.)

Earnest Shepherd Memorial Young Center Drama Day Camp, Junction of M-33 and U.S. 69, Liberty, MO 64068, 781-7733. (See Summer Camping Programs under Great Outdoors.)

Linda Lovan Community School of Music, William Jewell College, Liberty, MO 64068, 781-7700, Ext. 426. Music lessons in everything from trumpet and tuba to guitar and saxophone are offered here. *Ages:* all. *Important to Know:* ($) (B)

Liberty Symphony Orchestra, P.O. Box 30, Liberty, MO 64068, 781-7700. More than 70 musicians perform together, usually at Gano Hall at William Jewell College during the year and offer an annual concert for pre-school and grade school children. *Important to Know:* ($) (B)

Ruth Stocksdale Gallery of Art, Brown Hall, William Jewell College, Liberty, MO 64068, 781-7700, Ext. 5413. The exhibits, which change monthly, are often of interest for children. Call before you go to see what's up. *Important to Know:* (No $) (B)

Liberty Civic Theater, P.O. Box 273, Liberty, MO 64068, **792-1192.** The theater group offers puppet shows such as "Three Little Pigs." The group meets monthly to plan productions and welcomes parents and children who want to take part. *Time Frame:* puppet shows take 15 minutes. *Ages:* pre-school and young elementary grades. *Important to Know:* (No $) (B, depending on where productions are given)

SPORTS

Mabee Center, William Jewell College, Liberty, MO 64068, 781-3806, Ext. 5299. The Mabee Center holds an Olympic-size indoor pool, and has volleyball, racketball, basketball and tennis. Family swim hours are offered all year. In summer, there are volleyball, basketball and football camps for kids. *Important to Know:* ($) (B)

Northland Rolladium Skate Center, 1020 Kent St. **(behind Wal-Mart), Liberty, MO 64068, 792-0590.** This rink holds beginning skating classes (except in summer) for children and adults. Family night is Tuesday. *Important to Know:* ($) (B)

THE GREAT OUTDOORS

Special Programs and Exhibits

Cumpton Park Zoo, 2 blocks E. of William Jewell College on Highway H, Liberty, MO 64068, 781-2800. This small, family-owned zoo features domestic and exotic animals that children can pet. A mini-train ride around the park takes about 5 minutes. *Ages:* all. *Important to Know:* The park is open on weekends, April through October. ($) (B) (D)

Liberty, Missouri, Parks and Recreation, 101 E. Kansas St., Liberty, MO 64068, 781-7100, Ext. 218. Classes in sports and gymnastics are offered. There are sports leagues, playground programs and more. *Ages:* 3 up. *Important to Know:* ($) (B) (D)

Special Area Parks and Playgrounds

The following parks and playgrounds offer wading pools, playground equipment, picnic shelters, horseshoe pits, lighted ball fields and more. For a more complete listing phone the Liberty, Missouri, Parks and Recreation (see Assistance, Liberty, MO.).

Bennett Park, Clayview and Spruce Streets, north of M-152. This 45-acre park also features an amphitheater, tennis and volleyball courts, concession stand and fitness trail.

City Park, M-291 and Moss St.

Russell Stocksdale Park, LaFrenz Rd., south of Richfield Rd. Here you'll find beautiful hiking trails along a wilderness area.

Ruth Moore Park, Between Morse and Grover Sts.

Westboro-Centerbury Greenway, Park Lane, south of Liberty Dr. The park has an asphalt trail.

Nature Sanctuaries

Martha LaFite Thompson nature Sanctuary, 407 N. LaFrenz Rd., (1/2 mile S.E. of William Jewell College), Liberty, MO 64068, 781-8598. This 100-acre sanctuary is filled with wildlife that inhabits prairie, woodland, meadow and marsh habitats. White-tailed deer, raccoons, foxes, squirrels, birds and butterflies delight the eyes. The Visitor Center features educational exhibits for children and has organized activities such as wildflower and full-moon hikes. *Ages:* Pre-schoolers should be able to walk a mile-long trail. *Important to Know:* comfy walking shoes a must. No pets and no perfume, since it attracts bees. (I) (G/R) (No $) (B)

Summer Camping Programs

Earnest Shepherd Memorial Young Center Drama Day Camp, Junction of M-33 and U.S. 69, Liberty, MO 64068, 781-7733. This drama day camp teaches acting and technical skills and improvisational technique to children in a large air-conditioned building. Kids get lunch and can swim during the day. *Ages:* 4th to 8th grade. *Important to Know:* enrollment is limited to one week in summer, so reserve early. ($) (B)

Liberty Latchkey Summer Program, P.O. Box 120, Liberty, MO 64068, 792-1898. Weekly activities include Indian lore, campouts, field trips, arts and crafts, swimming, nature hikes, baseball and more. This excellent program has a better than average adult-to-child staffing ratio. *Ages:* 1st to 6th grade. *Important to Know:* registration is open to *all* Kansas City area residents. ($) (B)

Summer Sports Camps, Mabee Center, William Jewell College, Liberty, MO 64068, 781-7700, Ext. 5287. The center has volleyball and basketball camps for kids. *Ages:* 3 to 12. *Important to Know:* ($) (B)

SPECIAL ACTIVITIES

Young Achievers Program, William Jewell College, Liberty, MO 64068, 781-7700, Ext. 5395. Classes held during the academic year and in summer include computers, theater, creative writing, photography, languages, judo, gymnastics, clowning and more. *Ages:* 5 up. *Important to Know:* ($) (B)

Farmers Market, City of Liberty, City Hall, 101 E. Kansas St., Liberty, MO 64068, 781-7100. The market is open Saturdays around the courthouse square in downtown Liberty from May through late October. Children can pick out their own fruits and veggies. *Important to Know:* get there early; produce is sold out by mid-morning.

SPECIAL EVENTS CALENDAR

MAY

Spring on the Square, City of Liberty, Courthouse Square downtown, 101 E. Kansas St., Liberty, MO 64068, 781-7100. This spring event includes fine arts, crafts, antiques, and demonstrations by artisans. There are many activities planned for children, including story-telling and games of yesteryear. *Important to Know:* (No $)

SEPTEMBER

Liberty Fall Festival, Liberty Chamber of Commerce, 109 S. Leonard St., Liberty, MO 64068, 781-5200. This festival has food, arts and crafts, entertainment, kids' games and pony rides. A shuttle bus takes visitors around the seven commerce areas of town where activities are held. *Important to Know:* (No $) (D)

FUN EATS

Perkins Restaurants, 781-0355. (See Listing under restaurants for Clay County, Kansas City, MO.)

Winsteads, Crossroads Shopping Center, junction of M-291 and M-152, Liberty, MO 64068, 792-3444. (Check your phone book for other Winstead's locations around Greater Kansas City.) Burgers, sodas, malts and sundaes are offered, plus "Tiny Tot Meals" for the little ones.

PLATTE COUNTY, MISSOURI

KANSAS CITY NORTH, RIVERSIDE, PARKVILLE, PLATTE CITY,

KEY: (I) individual tours, no reservations needed; (I/R) individual tours, reservations needed; (G) group tours, no reservations needed; (G/R) group tours, reservations needed; ($) fee; (No $) no fee; (B) bathrooms; (No B) no bathrooms; (D) some accommodations for the disabled.

KANSAS CITY NORTH, RIVERSIDE, PARKVILLE, PLATTE CITY,

ASSISTANCE

Convention Bureaus and Chambers of Commerce

Parkville Chamber of Commerce, City Hall, Parkville, MO 64152, 741-7676.

Riverside Chamber of Commerce, 2901 N.W. Platte Rd., Riverside, MO 64150, 741-0452.

Platte County Business and Professional Association/Industrial Development Commission, 10920 Ambassador Drive, Kansas City, MO 64153, 891-9480.

Clubs and Organizations

Heart of America Council, Boy Scouts of America. (See Assistance, Kansas City, KS.)

Kansas City, Missouri, Council of Camp Fire. (See Assistance, East of Plaza, Kansas City, MO.)

Mid-Continent Council of Girl Scouts. (See Assistance, East of Plaza, Kansas City, MO.)

Clay-Platte YMCA, 1101 N.E. 47th St., Kansas City, MO 64116, 453-6600. The YMCA has an abundance of sports and cultural programs for kids, plus day camps, child care, and other offerings. Rather than trying to list them all in our limited space, we suggest calling for more information.

Special Assistance—Day Care

Division of Family Services. (See Assistance, Downtown Kansas City, MO.)

YWCA Resource and Referral. (See Assistance, Downtown Kansas City, MO.)

Special Assistance for the Disabled

Direction Service Center. (See Special Assistance for the Disabled, Independence, MO.)

The Whole Person, Inc. (See Listing under Special Assistance for the Disabled, South of Plaza, Kansas City, MO.)

Transportation

Mayflower Contract Services, P.O. Box 14008, 6207 N.W. Bell, Parkville, MO 64152, 741-4023. The company offers service to Royals Games from Kansas City North area. Children 5 and under ride free.

Parks and Recreation Departments

Parks and Recreation Department, 8509 N.W. Stagecoach, Kansas City, MO 64154, 436-4886.

BUSINESS AND COMMERCIAL TOURS

Kansas City Aviation Department, KCI Airport, 121 Paris St., Kansas City, MO 64195, 243-5244. Children can visit one of the three terminal buildings, the operations and maintenance center and the Aircraft, Rescue, Firefighting Facility. *Time Frame:* 30 minutes. *Ages:* K up. *Important to Know:* (I/R) (G/R) (No $) (B) (D)

Platte County Area Vocational Technical School, M-92, P.O. Box 1400, Platte City, MO 64089, 816-464-5505. This tour takes in a discussion of career and vocational education. Kids get a chance to see classes in data processing, computer programming, electronics, food service, building trades and more. *Time Frame:* 45 minutes. *Ages:* 7th and 8th grades. *Important to Know:* (G/R) (No $) (B) (D)

Pizza Hut, 6411 N.W. 72nd St., Kansas City, MO 64151, 587-8150. Children get to see what waitresses and cooks do. They watch the cook preparing and baking pizzas, and youngsters get to make their very own personal pan pizza. *Time Frame:* one and a half hours. *Ages:* 4 up. *Important to Know:* (G/R) (No $ for pizza-making; drinks extra) (B)

Platte County Courthouse, 324 Main St., Platte City, MO 64089, 816-464-2232. Children learn about county government and view the county communication, police dispatching and county computer systems, and jail when the deputies are available. *Time Frame:* 30 minutes. *Ages:* 2nd grade up. *Important to Know:* (I/R) (G/R) (No $) (B) (D)

TWA Overhaul Base, I-29 and 112th St., Kansas City, MO 64195, 891-4940. There's a guided tour of the hangar and kids can view aircraft undergoing maintenance and overhaul work. *Time Frame:* 2 hours. *Ages:* minimum age is 12 years. *Important to Know:* call well in advance. Don't bring cameras and come prepared to walk a lot. One adult must accompany every 10 children. (G/R) (No $) (B)

HISTORIC SITES AND MUSEUMS

Ben Ferrel Platte County Museum, Corner of Ferrell and Third Sts., one block south of Courthouse Square, Platte City, MO 816-431-5121. Completed in 1883, this Victorian home once owned by Frederick Krause, his wife and seven children, has been restored and is open to the public. The house is decorated for special Christmas tours and the children's rooms are furnished with toys and games. *Time Frame:* 30 minutes. *Ages:* 5 up. *Important to Know:* (G/R) ($) (B)

Line Creek Archaeological Museum, 5940 N.W. Waukomis Drive, Kansas City, MO 64151, 444-4363. (Also see The Great Outdoors.) The museum, located on the grounds of Line Creek Park, has tours of a life-size replica of a pre-historic Hopewell Indian village along with a slide presentation and lecture. The museum also offers classes in Indian pottery-making and Hopewell Indian culture for older kids. School groups can also participate in archaeological digs at the Hopewell Indian site. The park also has nature and hiking areas, buffalo, deer and other wildlife. *Ages:* 4th grade up. *Important to Know:* call ahead for museum days and hours. (I) (G/R) ($) (B)

Park College, Parkville, MO 64152, 741-2000. Mackay Hall, completed in 1893, was built by students who hand-hewed limestone and hauled it up ramps to fashion the structure. You can take a self-guided tour of the grounds, and listen to the 135-foot clock tower's carillon chimes that ring the quarter hours. This can be your first stop on your visit to Parkville. *Ages:* 2nd grade up. *Important to Know:* (I) (G) (No $) (B)

THE ARTS

Young Audiences Arts Card,™ Kansas City Chapter of Young Audiences. (See The Arts, Midtown Kansas City, MO.)

Bell Road Barn Players, David Community Theatre, 4200 W. Riverside St., Riverside, MO 64150, 587-0218. The oldest community theater in Kansas City stages several productions annually. Children are more apt to enjoy the comedies and musicals. *Time Frame:* performances are 2 hours. *Ages:* 8 up. *Important to Know:* ($) (B)

Children's Summer Art Program, Parkville Fine Arts Assn., 164 S. Main, Parkville Landing, Parkville, MO 64152, 741-7270. Certified art instructors lead weekday sessions in drawing, clay work, watercolors, batik, jewelry making and other arts and crafts. After class, art is displayed in Parkville's Country Gallery (see below). *Ages:* 7 to 12. *Important to Know:* classes fill up fast, so register early. ($) (B)

Country Gallery in Parkville, Parkville Landing, South Main St., Parkville, MO 64152, 741-7270. Works by Midwestern artists are represented here, from paintings, pottery and photography to mixed media pieces. Children are invited to meet with the artists at a public reception held each month. The gallery also displays work by youngsters who participate in Parkville's summer art program. *Ages:* 7 up. *Important to Know:* don't forget to check out some of the other Parkville Landing galleries. (No entrance $) (B)

Northland Symphony Orchestra, P.O. Box 12255, Kansas City, MO 64152, 741-4221. The company of 70 players was formed in 1968 as a community orchestra. The group performs Sunday concerts in Park Hill High School auditorium at 7701 N.W. Barry Rd. The program consists of classical music that is unusually familiar to children. *Time Frame:* concerts run one and a half hours. *Ages:* 2nd grade up. *Important to Know:* (No $) (B) (D)

Philharmonia of Greater Kansas City, P.O. Box 14448, Parkville, MO 64152, 587-2920. (Also see Playing Together.) The company gives several performances annually in the Graham Tyler Memorial Chapel at Park College. The concerts are family-oriented, with Halloween and Christmas offerings containing popular holiday music familiar to children. *Time Frame:* concerts run 2 hours. *Ages:* 8 up. *Important to Know:* (No $) (B)

AMUSEMENTS

Bell Museum, Red X General Store, junction of M-9, U.S. 169 and U.S. 69, Riverside, MO 64150, 741-3377. Ed Young, who owns the store, claims one of the most amazing and largest collections of bells in the world. Kids are allowed to touch and ring many of the 10,000 bells, some of which once hung from Conestoga wagons and Oriental temples. *Ages:* all. *Important to Know:* (No $) (B)

Coachlite Skate Center, 4720 N.W. Gateway, Riverside, NO 64150, 741-1226. This roller skating center is open on weekends and provides family-oriented fun. Call for times. *Ages:* all. *Important to Know:* ($) (B)

Ralph's Antique Dolls, 7 Main St., Parkville, MO 64152, 741-3120. Ralph Griffith has about 500 unusual or antique dolls on display and for sale in the shop, from those with two faces to dolls who look like famous people. *Ages:* all. *Important to Know:* (No $ to enter) (No B)

Stable T Farm for Kids, 10301 N.W. Blum Rd., Kansas City, MO 64152, 741-1058. Ron and Patti Tilman's 20-acre pasture houses about 90 animals. They offer field trips, horsemanship classes and weekend trail rides on their farm. Children get to see domestic animals and assorted critters that they can pet and touch. Wiener roasts and scavenger hunts are part of the trail ride fun. This makes an entertaining birthday outing. *Ages:* kids through age 12. *Important to Know:* (G/R) ($) (B) (D)

SPORTS

Kansas City, Missouri, Parks and Recreation Department. For a listing of various parks, community centers, sports activities, and camping programs in the Greater Kansas City area phone 274-1671, 444-3113.

Snow Creek Ski Lodge, Box 258, Weston, MO 64089, near 45 Highway, south of Weston, 816-386-2200. The lodge is available to skiers from mid-December through mid-March. Snow Creek features 12 slopes, a lodge and restaurant, rental shop, chair lifts and night skiing. On weekends, a kiddie area is sectioned off for a two-hour lesson visited by cartoon characters. This is a good way to teach children how to ski. *Ages:* old enough to stand on skis. *Important to Know:* ($) (B)

PLAYING TOGETHER

Summer Orchestra, Philharmonia of Greater Kansas City, P.O. Box 14448, Parkville, MO 64152, 587-2920. In summer, as a community service, the Philharmonia and Park College sponsor a Summer Orchestra which is open to players of all ages and skill levels without audition. Parents and children may join the group to perform together. The orchestra meets weekly in June and gives a concert in late summer. *Ages:* 7 up. *Important to Know:* (No $) (B)

THE GREAT OUTDOORS

Special Programs and Exhibits

Frank Vaydik-Line Creek Park, 5940 N.W. Waukomis, **Kansas City, MO 64151, 741-7201.** The 122-acre park contains the Line Creek Archaeology Museum, an animal enclosure for buffalo and elk, ball diamonds, and Line Creek. The grounds are on the site where the prehistoric Hopewell Indians lived and the museum contains a lifesize diorama of a Hopewell Village as well as artifacts from the era. Programs, including archaeological digs where children can participate, are featured. *Ages:* all. *Important to Know:* (No $) (B)

Special Area Parks and Playgrounds

Most area parks offer picnic areas, ball fields, tennis courts, playgrounds, shelters and more. This is a sampling of what you'll find:

Barry-Platte Park, take Barry Rd. 3 miles E. of I-29, then 1/4 mile N. on Old Stagecoach Rd., Kansas City, MO 64155. This is close to Metro North Mall. (D)

English Landing Park, near the riverfront, southeast of historic downtown Parkville, Parkville, MO 64152, 741-7676. Especially of interest is an 1898 truss bridge.

Summer Camping Programs

Fishing and Hunter Education Camp, Game Hill Summer Camp, 9802 Marsh, Kansas City, MO 64134, 761-

7095. Children learn hunting and fishing skills in this unusual one-week resident camp offered in Weston, MO. Courses in wild-game cooking, gun safety, black powder shooting, taxidermy, fishing skills, turkey and deer hunting, canoeing and conservation are given. Graduates receive a certificate in Missouri Hunter Education from the Missouri Department of Conservation. *Ages:* 10 to 15. *Important to Know:* ($) (B)

SPECIAL ACTIVITIES

Line Creek Archaeological Museum, 5940 N.W. Waukomis Drive, Kansas City, MO 64151, 444-4363. (See The Great Outdoors and Historic Sites and Museums, this section.)

Parkville Farmers Market, at the foot of East St., near English Landing Park, contact City Hall, Parkville, MO 64152, 741-7676. On Saturdays from May through early fall, the farmer's market is loaded with vendors selling everything from produce and plants to baked goods. Kids can pick out their own fruits and vegetables to take home. We recommend starting your morning here, checking out the nearby shops, and stopping for a soda at McKeon's on Main Street. If kids get tired, there's a playground and restrooms in English Landing Park.

SPECIAL EVENTS CALENDAR

MAY

Parkville May Fest, City of Parkville and Parkville Chamber of Commerce, Parkville, MO 64152, 741-7676. Held in the historic downtown district, this family-oriented event includes a parade, contests, music, food and entertainment. *Important to Know:* (No $)

SEPTEMBER

Parkville Days, Parkville Chamber of Commerce and the City of Parkville, City Hall, Parkville, MO 64152, 741-7676. This festival comes complete with a parade, music, food, entertainment, and games for all age groups. *Important to Know:* (No $)

FUN EATS

Papa Frank's Restaurant, 103 Main St., Parkville, MO 64152, 587-1516. This popular family restaurant has good food and a reasonably priced children's menu. (D)

Stephenson's Apple Tree Inn, 5755 Northwood Rd., off I-29, Kansas City, MO 64151, 587-9300. Kids get a chance at Stephenson's, where they can order from their own whimsical menu that features such items as a Smokey-Wokey, Piggy Wiggy and Little Red Hen. A country store on the premises sells candy, stuffed animals and Midwestern food favorites. Free cider is served inside the door. (D)

GOODIES

McKeon's Party Shop, 15 Main St., Parkville, MO 64152, 741-9835. This authentic old-fashioned soda fountain is located in a liquor store and has yesterday's prices on ice cream sundaes, sodas and more. *Important to Know:* (D)

A Kid's Guide to Kansas City

ADVENTURE COUPONS

**Use these coupons and enjoy savings
on food, sightseeing, kids' clothes and more!**

A Kid's Guide to Kansas City
ADVENTURE COUPONS

A Kid's Guide to Kansas City
ADVENTURE COUPONS

A Kid's Guide to Kansas City
ADVENTURE COUPONS

A Kid's Guide to Kansas City
ADVENTURE COUPONS

A Kid's Guide to Kansas City

ADVENTURE COUPONS

A Kid's Guide to Kansas City

ADVENTURE COUPONS

A Kid's Guide to Kansas City

ADVENTURE COUPONS

A Kid's Guide to Kansas City

ADVENTURE COUPONS

A Kid's Guide to Kansas City
ADVENTURE COUPONS

A Kid's Guide to Kansas City
ADVENTURE COUPONS

A Kid's Guide to Kansas City
ADVENTURE COUPONS

A Kid's Guide to Kansas City
ADVENTURE COUPONS

Author, publisher and travel correspondent, Shifra Stein is the creator of the nationally-acclaimed "Day Trips America" series. Her popular guides have been published for several cities including Kansas City, Houston, Baltimore and Phoenix-Tucson-Flagstaff. Her other books include "Kansas City: A Unique Guide to the Metro Area," "The All-American Barbecue Book," and "All About Bar-B-Q: Kansas City-Style." Ms. Stein is also a syndicated broadcaster whose radio show, "TravelTalk," is currently aired over 130 stations on the WAXWORKS network. A member of the prestigious Society of American Travel Writers, Ms. Stein's work has appeared in numerous newspapers and magazines including *The Los Angeles Times, New York Daily News, Midwest Living,* and others. When she's not on the road, Ms. Stein makes her home in Kansas City.

BOYS & GIRLS CLUBS OF GREATER KANSAS CITY

Because of "Kid's Guide's" emphasis on fun, exploratory opportunities for young people and their families, Harrow Books is pleased to contribute a portion of proceeds from specified sales of this book to The Boys & Girl's Clubs of Greater Kansas City. Area readers might wish to consider their own gift to the organization, which has a long history of service to inner city youth.

The Boys & Girls Clubs of Greater Kansas City is a non-profit youth organization providing service to approximately 3000 children ages 7 to 17 in the inner city.

The mission of the Clubs is juvenile delinquency prevention and positive youth development directed especially to children from disadvantaged backgrounds. The Clubs aim to help children "beat the streets."

Programs include cultural arts, college work scholarship, job training & placement, computer education, individual and team sports, learning centers, free breakfasts and lunches, leadership clubs, and the world famous Marching Cobras!

The Boys & Girls Clubs hopes that the children who visit the many places described in "Kids Guide to Kansas City" have many hours of enjoyment, laughter and discovery. Many of the children who live in the inner city may not have these opportunities. Please help the Boys & Girls Clubs offer those opportunities to our inner city kids with a gift of your time or dollars.

The Boys & Girls Clubs of Greater Kansas City
3200 Wayne   Kansas City, Mo. 64109
(816) 923-1232

Coming from
Harrow Books
Fall, 1989

FOCUS KANSAS CITY:
A 24 HOUR HEARTLAND PORTRAIT

This 9" x 12" photodocumentary volume in full color details the way Kansas Citians work, play, govern, educate and amuse themselves in some 250 photographs taken by 117 photographers from midnight to midnight on Oct. 5, 1988. The results of the largest single-day photo project in Kansas City's history, inspired by "A Day in the Life of America," will touch your heart and your funnybone.

KANSAS CITY SEASONS
1990 Engagement Calendar

Area bookstores and gift shops nearly sold out of the 1989 version of this calendar that was initiated last fall. This year, well-known Kansas City photographer Roy Inman's singular imagery will guide the viewer through the richness of the four seasons in America's heartland capital.

THE PLAZA

Kansas City's fabled shopping district in all its beauty and diversity is the subject of this large, four-color volume that includes text and pictures revealing its historic past and vibrant present. The breath-taking beauty of its architecture, the fast pace of its stylish shops and boutiques, the luxuriousness of its residential environment are captured in principal photography by Bob Barrett. Writers Dory DeAngelo and Shifra Stein provide the words to go with the pictures.

RAPTOR RAPTURE/THE OWLS OF AMERICA
1990 Engagement Calendar

Held in awe, admiration and apprehension, the owl is one of this country's proudest and most misunderstood birds. At once majestic and mysterious, there are surprisingly few species of owls remaining on the North American continent. This collection of photographs and accompanying test reveal the dramatic beauty of these winged creatures of the night.

GAS-SAVING GETAWAYS LESS THAN TWO HOURS FROM YOUR DOOR!

DAY TRIPS A New Travel Book That Gives You Over 200 Exciting Places To Visit, Easily. Reached On A Tank Or Two Of Gas!

Mini-Vacations—including cities, towns, historical museums, residences, homes tours, galleries, antique shops, a tropical rain forest, state parks and historic sites, campgrounds, celebrations, festivals, wildlife refuges, restaurants and much more (location and hours given).

Restaurants—DAY TRIPS is also a restaurant guide, listing fine, moderately priced establishments where you can dine in comfort in your travels. Some of these spots have historical significance.

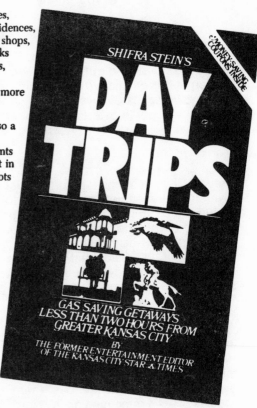

SHIFRA STEIN'S

DAY TRIPS

MONEY-SAVING COUPONS INSIDE

GAS SAVING GETAWAYS LESS THAN TWO HOURS FROM GREATER KANSAS CITY

BY THE FORMER ENTERTAINMENT EDITOR OF THE KANSAS CITY STAR & TIMES

"AN ODE TO THE BACKROADS OF MISSOURI AND KANSAS"
... Kansas City Star Newspaper

AVAILABLE AT BOOKSTORES!